Down a Cobbled Street

First published in 1987 by Badger Books.
Reprinted 1994, 1997, 2001
Typeset by Lens Typesetting, Bideford.
Printed by Maslands Ltd., Tiverton

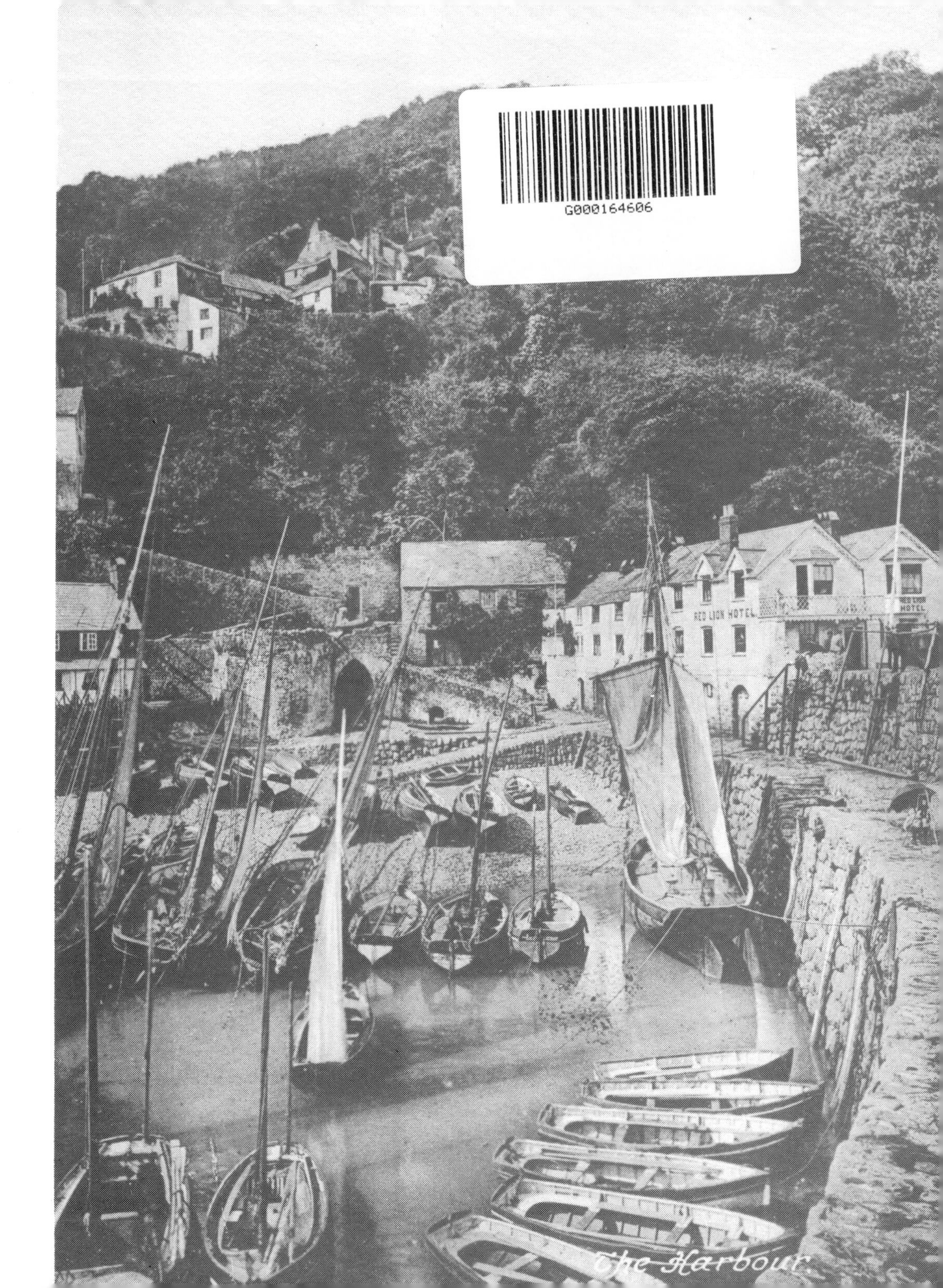

DOWN A COBBLED STREET

The work of Paul Ashton Ellis is well known and sought after in this corner of North Devon. His daughter, Sheila Ellis, wanted his photographs to reach a wider public, and with the writing of her book, she has achieved a lifelong ambition.

Paul Ellis was born in Clovelly in 1902. As a result of a childhood accident he was a semi-invalid, and took up photography as a way of earning a living. He married Gladys Braund from Bucks Mills in 1925 and together they opened a small newsagents and photographic business in the front room of White Cottage. Sheila was born two years later, and remembers following her father around as he set up his tripod to take the evocative and excellent pictures that form the bulk of this book. Both her parents died in 1965, and the vast collection, much of it mounted on glass plates, was carefully stored. Sheila Ellis closed the shop in 1975 and formed what she calls the "Clovelly Room" – a treasure house of memorabilia, including her father's photographs as well as many taken by herself and other members of her family. They have proved of great interest to countless friends and visitors (although not on view to the general public).

She has, over the years, collected together the reminiscences of many of her friends and neighbours and with this book records Clovelly as she and many others remember it.

The author when very young.

Clovelly – steep cobbled pathway, cottages on either side – smothered in flowers, and the sea ahead. This is the scene conjured up when the name is mentioned!

Maybe Clovelly is famous the world over; it **is** very beautiful, to say the least. Many folk visit it every year, and many guide-books have been written and so our fame will continue to spread. I do not attempt to make another, but to draw attention to the origin and background of this community, plus a few dates of interest, a few local events, some of it's people, and a little about it's cottages. But first we shall need to travel back a long, long way, and eventually we shall catch up and come right back to the present day.

We are situated in a valley on the north coast of Devon. The sea ahead is known either as "Clovelly" or "Bideford Bay," and to the west, the Atlantic. Opposite, on the far shore, we see two headlands, Morte Point and Baggy Point, treacherous landmarks for all ships, with many caves which can be seen from a boat. Eastwards from Morte Point lies Ilfracombe. Across the bay we see the large whitewashed hotel at Saunton with its 365 windows, practically built on the sandhills.

The estuary of the rivers Taw and Torridge flows into the bay, its mouth blocked by The Bar, a huge sand bank which is such a tiresome worry to all who go in and out by boat. Above the two estuaries the sun rises and the bay is a glorious sight on a summer morning, bathed in rosy-red and gold. Travelling along the last stretch of the rocky arm which surrounds and protects us, we have red sandstone cliffs with green grass above. Even the cliffs have names, Greencliff, Cockington, Portledge and Peppercombe.

The main road from Bideford to Bude is woven into this large curve, and passes the top of Bucks Mills which, like us, is set into the rock-side. About one mile from Bucks Cross is the entrance to Hobby Drive, one of our boundaries. We can either travel through or continue on the main road, passing Burnstone, Eastacott and Holiwell Farms, and the old Hobby Drive entrance, all on the right. To the left lie Downland and Slade Farms, and finally, the turning to Woolsery. We reach Dyke Green, – a filling station, cottages, and behind, the famous iron age earth works known as the Dykes. Then comes Turnpikegate, as it once was, and Higher Clovelly. To the right, Winsworthy Council Estate, and the hamlet of Burscot with Police House, a farm, and more cottages, old and new.

A few yards down the steep main road are Slerra cottages, and a turning to the right, where we find the Parish hall, the school and six dwellings, set in Wrinkleberry. Down even further, and ahead are the iron gates to Clovelly Court. Home Lodge is on the left, and the Parish Church peeps out between the trees. Finally, we travel past the Rectory on the right, and come to a small car-park, and below the famous cobbled street – for pedestrians only!

As for the village, we do know that the present lay-out dates from the 1600's, but to describe it clearly before that is not possible. We continually mourn the fact that fire has destroyed practically all the Clovelly records; the manor house held all local and ecclesiastical documents. It has been stated that a pier was in place hundreds of years before George Cary is said to have built

Taken over 100 years ago – the stream emptied onto the beach on the extreme left – where the Lifeboat House is now.

his pier; it is much more likely that he enlarged or extended an existing structure. He made a good job in the valley, however. A river ran from a point up in the woods, almost in Higher Clovelly. It twisted and turned on its way down to the sea.

"So the brilliant George had cottages built on either side, beginning at the beach and working upwards. Afterwards the water was diverted to a pathway through the woods and down the cliffside to the beach. All this cost £2,000. (His Will of 1611 quotes this). Much later, thousands of cobbles were carried up from the beach and laid across the now dry river bed."
(Making of the English Landscape – Prof. W.G. Hoskins).

A small stream of water still ran on the right-side, and tiny bridges crossed to the cottages. This remained so until 1861, when a cholera epidemic occurred. Charles Kingsley was staying at Bideford, and chanced to be strolling down one day. He pounced on this smelly stream as the culprit in which everything foul and dangerous was flowing. The owners of Clovelly at that time were the Hamlyns. They arranged for cobbles to be carted up, and the water was covered in. It still flows to this day, under cottages on the right (below the New Inn), under a stretch of street, down again under Nos. 79 and 78, across another piece of cobbling, under the cliff, through a cleft, and out into the street above the Bow. Time was when it emptied on the beach, but that was when a larger amount of water flowed. Here is an extract about Clovelly written between 1534 and 1543 by John Leland, the famous traveller.

"Bytwix the mouth of Tawe and Hertey Point, lyith a very cumpasid bay, and almost in the middle thereof is a place called "Clovelle", whereabout Cary dwellith and here is the nearest trajectus in to Lundey Isle". (He speaks of Robert Cary who died in 1540.) Again – "At Clovelly there is a little pier for vessels and the harbour is noted for the herring fishery. The land as it juts out into the promontory of Hartland, is by no means remarkable for fertility, nor is it either nove, or varied enough to be pleasinf to the eye".
(Observations of Western Counties: W.G. Maton 1794-6).

The cobbled street before the stream was covered in.

Not very flattering, but nice to know that we were worth a paragraph or two!! It was during this period that Clovelly as we know it began to take shape. The pier was lengthened in 1826, cottages re-built or restored, parkland was created and thousands of trees planted. Beautiful walks were cut out of the land, and paths made along the cliff-edge. Tiny shelters were built or carved – "The Cabin", "The Wilderness", "Angels' Wings", delightful names and charming spots. A gate near the top of the Turnpike road is the entrance to this park which is private.

The Summerhouse above Mouth Mill built in 1820 and restored in 1935 for Christine Hamlyn's 80th birthday.

Angels Wings.

A cove, Mouth Mill, is tucked away at the end of one path, rugged and wild, and a stream tumbles down into the sea. A lime-kiln (a double of the one in Clovelly harbour), stands idle now. Time was when boats came in from South Wales loaded with limestone and culm. This culm was a poor type of fuel, and formed the fire to burn the limestone. When the powdered lime was cold, it was loaded on donkeys and sold to farmers to fertilise the land, this being the cheapest type in those days. (Seaweed was also used in coastal areas). The kilns were last fired in 1911.

Around the rocky headland toward Clovelly, we see a steep cliff, Gallantry Bower, four hundred feet high.

Mouth Mill – cottages adjoining the lime kiln, now partially demolished.

"The Mary" unloads coal at Mouth Mill.

London Lodge – the original entrance to the Hobby.

Hobby Drive

One of the loveliest walks is along The Hobby Drive, laid out by the Hamlyns between 1811 and 1829; the work was carried out by local men. Trees, ferns and mossy banks are to be enjoyed all the way from Hobby Lodge to Clovelly. Four gently curving bridges cross streams, and each one brings us nearer to habitation again. Lovely views of the bay and coastline are glimpsed, and seats wait invitingly. The track is rugged. Cars may be driven through, but care must be taken on the sharp bends. April-May is bluebell time, and the sun shines through on a haze of blue and green, our beloved birds sing – it feels like heaven.

From the Hobby seat.

"Steepways" taken from near the first bridge.

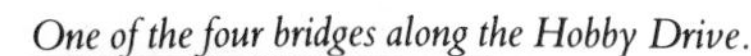

One of the four bridges along the Hobby Drive.

Down a Cobbled Street

Flowers grow super-abundantly in our climate, that is, unless an east or north-east wind blows too often and burns them. Honeysuckle scents the air on a summer evening, fuschias in many varieties thrive and in places are used as hedges. Hydrangeas, pink, blue and white, love it here, but the gayest of all flowers are the geraniums, mainly the scarlet "Paul Crampnel", but the ivy-leaved group also do well. All tall and delicate plants are protected in winter; usually sheets of plastic are tied and tacked around them. Visitors gaze in awe at the plants climbing the cottage walls. None survived the 1962-63 blizzard, so all present plants are replacements. Almost everyone has a floral path in front of their cottage; even a narrow border can look charming, and gay pots and tubs stand where no garden exists.

In the 1870's, and for many years afterwards, artists sat patiently on little stools in the High Street, painting the beauty all around them; not only the main street, but also the side turnings with names like Fish Street, Independent Street, Providence Row, Back Lane, Back Side, and North Hill. The "Look-out" is a flat area, with a superb view over the harbour and bay. Likewise the quay, and view from the old pier, – everywhere a scene to paint, nowadays to photograph. My grandfather came regularly to Clovelly to paint. He stayed at No. 9 or ("Jessamine Cottage") now called "Kingsley Cottage", as Charles also stayed there. He, John Ellis, married Alice Jewell, "the daughter of the house", in 1900. My father, Paul, was born in this cottage, in the room in which Charles Kingsley had written part of "Westward Ho!". They moved to No. 11 in 1902 calling it "The White Cottage" and were the first tenants after restoration.

Providence Row.

North Hill Cottage—the late Mr. J. T. Moss with the author.

Independent Street.

Fish Street.

So we see Clovelly in the 1980's, and realise how lucky we are to live in such a wonderful spot. Some of us were born here, (I live in the same cottage), some chose to settle here, and a few decided to retire here. After the hustle and bustle of the big towns, living here is another world, though climbing up the steep, cobbled street presents a problem as we grow older.

A lot of people ask the same questions during the course of a season:- "What do you do in the winter?" "However do you manage the hill?" "How do you get supplies of food, coal, beer?" "How does anyone move furniture in or out?" "How much does a cottage cost?" "What happens when someone is ill – dies?" "Does it ever snow?" "Do you have a doctor, policeman, church, chapel, school, bus-service, postal delivery and collection?"
Well, we keep our faces as straight as possible, and give the best answers we can. Most food items can be purchased at the village store and post office, but a trip to Bideford makes a change now and then. Shopping baskets hang heavily by the time we have walked from the bus-stop at the higer car-park. Then a small sledge comes in useful. These are of wood, rather like a wide ladder on runners. Almost all householders have one, to bring down goods or coal. Larger models are used to drag down fruit, vegetables and groceries to the shop; bread supplies twice weekly; beer and other drinks to the New Inn; and laundry. A special sledge with two handles is used to bring luggage down to the hotel. This is the original type, and heavier.

Until recently refuse was tipped from our buckets into large bins strapped onto a sledge, pulled to the bottom of the village, and removed by a Council lorry next day, but now plastic sacks are delivered to each cottage at Christmas and at Midsummer and someone collects our filled bags each week.

Coal is delivered in discarded animal-food bags filled with several types of fuel, and about ten sacks are placed on a sledge and delivered from house to house. Many cottages are heated by electricity, as it is so much easier than humping buckets of coal and disposing of the endless ashes afterwards.

Milk now arrives in stiff plastic cartons; before that, in thin plastic bags, and they felt like frozen fish! Milk bottles were tried out, but dozens were broken the first day. The suppliers, before "packed" milk came along, would milk their own cows, fill two churns or cans with handles, place a yoke across their shoulders, suspend the two cans from it, and walk down from Higher Clovelly. They delivered from door to door, dipping up a half or one-pint measure of milk for everyone.

Dustbin day – the late Ernest Beer collecting refuse.

Donkey-power – beer and milk.

Coal delivery, 1980.

1960's and an easier method of delivery.

Rolling barrels – the hard way to deliver beer. The coronation picture below the inn sign dates the picture as 1937.

Bread delivery men and boys congregate look out

Two butchers bring meat from door to door twice a week. Their burden is very heavy as they leave the car-park to start their rounds, but they swing along on their way back up again, with empty baskets. Our postal service is still pretty good – two deliveries and collections each weekday except Saturday. In the old days, a donkey carried the mail up. A man and woman walked or cycled the entire post round of the parish. They covered hundreds of miles over our huge rural area, and the woman, when over 80, could keep a roomful of listeners happy by telling her "post-girl tales".

Coffins have always been carried to the Parish Church, six bearers at a time, changing to another six every few yards. Now a hearse usually waits at the end of the cobbles, and in any case, more people die in hospital than in the days of old. Usually, a "body comes home" and rests overnight in church.

An ambulance can now reverse to the Fountain, a flat platform before the cobbled ridges begin. This is an improvement, as someone can become ill when our men are out at work, and helpers are not as plentiful as they were to carry a patient up. It's a bumpy ride up in the ambulance though. I escorted my parents on two occasions, so speak from experience.

We have a sedan-type chair for slightly ill folk, and need four men to carry this up. Our doctor can drive his car to the Fountain too, and has arrived in minutes to attend very sick patients. No-one else may legally drive on this track. It is only a cobbled lane, and was not constructed for motor traffic. The doctor's surgery is held in a cottage lying three-quarters of the way down the street, No. 73. Here, on a Monday evening or Thursday morning, ailing folk meet, to pour out their troubles, first to the nearest listener, and then to the doctor! The wooden fruit carving which surrounds the door and is also fixed over the bay window, was purchased by Mrs. Hamlyn in Oberammergau in 1910 and shipped home. The following year, another set arrived for No. 37 which is situated around the corner at "Back side". This pleasant house sits right on the cliff-edge, a sheer drop to the harbour below. Many years ago, three small thatched cob cottages occupied this ground. One fell over the cliff, and two were re-made into this new dwelling, completed in 1912. Cliff Cottage, some yards away is also perched on a rocky ledge. This is a newer version of a cottage which had stood there for centuries.

"Back Side" – Oberammergau carving – and the author.

The Look Out Cottage, Bow or Temple Bar and Red Lion, from Independent St.

Looking down the valley, we see Temple Bar or The Bow, two cottages joined, and one stretching across the street making an unusual archway beneath. An old shoe-maker once dwelt in a minute cottage adjoining; this is now a cellar.

Continue with me a few yards more and we see the lime-kiln, down by the harbour. Small boats usually lie nearby, inside a gate. Boat trips are very popular, and fishing parties are catered for, as well. It is a good way to relax. Swimming is pleasant when the tide fills the harbour, as the water is more settled inside the arm of the pier. Along the shore-line, much slippery seaweed lies, and the current can be quite powerful when the tide is out. Several very low tide levels per year give us a gorgeous stretch of sand. Oh! if only we could hold back the sea and always find it! Angling has become a popular sport. Many fishermen come and stand all night in all weathers, hoping for a bite.It is quite usual to hear them tramping up the cobbles in the small hours, swinging an old-fashioned lantern.

Oberammergau carving—No. 73.

Back row: *Miss Margary May (now Mrs. Allin), Peggy Jennings, Barbara Day, Susan Cook, Doreen Braund, Faith Cruse, Ronnie Williams;* middle row: *Molly Beer, Betty Cook, Mary Littlejohns, Florrie Jewel, Margaret Jewell;* front row: *Tom Cruse, Les Rowe (RIP), George Smith, Caleb Jennings, Bill Rowe, Burnard Abbot (RIP).*

St. Peter's Chapel (1960c).

The school was opened in 1873. Many more families lived here then – the population was around 900, with anything up to ten children per family. Wrinkleberry was chosen for the site, which was a long walk from the outlying farms, and also from the harbour. Unless a child carried a packet of food for the mid-day break, it meant walking home at least a mile to the quay – four miles each day! Prior to this there had been a Charity School for girls run by Lady Hamlyn; pew-rents brought forth £3 per year towards the upkeep of the school.

A boys' school was in the hands of a Mr Dannell, who boasted that he had taught Charles Kingsley, and was held in what is now St Peter's Chapel in Providence Row. The chapel was licensed in 1846 by the Bishop of Exeter "for those residents not able to climb the hill to attend the Parish Church". In 1948, the former Rector, The Rev A S Chandler, had the same idea, not knowing of the earlier dedication. We found the 1846 document a few winters ago.

Wrinkleberry school is only for the under-11's now. The older children travel to Bideford each day by bus, leaving at 8.00 a.m. and returning at 4.30 p.m., – a long day and almost 2,000 pupils in the school. The little ones are well-served until they reach this age-group.

War-time Clovelly

The war years brought many changes, and not all have happy memories. Clovelly Court was once again destroyed by fire, on 29th December, 1944. The last social event held in the Long Passage, (a huge, low room), being a whist drive on Boxing Night. The fire was terrible. I can still see the convalescing soldiers in their blue uniforms, and Mrs Asquith and her sister carrying treasures they had rescued from the blaze. Part of the Court has since been rebuilt.

Evacuees began to arrive in Clovelly in 1940–41, some before bombing became too bad, and later hundreds who had been lucky to escape. Teachers travelled with them, and we gained much from this period. Sadly the school register is incomplete and a lot of names have not been mentioned. The areas from which they came were Deptford, Peckham and Catford; also Bristol and Plymouth. The Plymouth children belonged to "Astor Hall" and lived at the New Inn, with helpers to care for them. School was packed – three classes were held in the hall and one in each classroom, but we took turns to attend, half a day each. Two other buildings held classes – the chapel, (now St. Peter's), and a room over the lifeboat house. The Rectory-room, situated near the Rectory gate, was fitted out as a kitchen, where a cook and assistant created delicious meals, and boys and girls marched down from Wrinkleberry to consume them. A domestic science mistress taught the older girls to cook and sew, while the older boys "dug for victory" in the gardens, one in Wrinkleberry Lane, and the other near the car park. Waste paper was collected too.

Food parcels were welcome. They came from the Commonwealth countries, and the Parish Council distributed gifts to the "over-70's". Warm, navy fisherman-type pullovers were knitted by a group of women, including Mrs Abbott and my mother. I remember grateful letters arriving from some of the sailors on *HMS Hood* and *Ark Royal*.

A searchlight battery was stationed at Woolsery Cross. A band of Home Guards met regularly at Mouth Mill and some of their experiences would make good material for the "Dad's Army" script-writers! Commandos were billetted around the parish, usually for two weeks at a time, two per household. They were training at Gallantry Bower, almost 400 feet high and their nightmares would be poured out to their landladies most of whom were more like mothers. A few survived the D-Day landing for which they were destined, and have returned to say "Thank-you" on several occasions.

Clovelly Court around 1930 – before the War time fire.

The village lost some men between 1939–45, but many more died in the 1914–18 war. Their names are engraved on a wall-plaque in the Parish Church. In 1943, it was decided to build a Memorial Hall to these men. A Committee was formed consisting of a representative from each organisation in the parish. Many years of fund-raising and site problems followed, until 1st October 1966 – opening day! It is used regularly, more often in winter than summer, when most people are engaged in catering for the needs of tourists.

Snow-covered Clovelly – a rare sight – 1962 and 1969.

In 1947 came the "Great Snow". Never before, and please God, never again! I suppose everyone remembers things which concerned them; here in Clovelly we endured much discomfort. Snowdrifts completely blocked all our roads, and we were cut off from Bideford, Bude and Hartland. No supplies came through until a pathway had been shovelled by hard-working men – no snow-ploughs then. My uncle, a baker, hired a horse and cart, piled fresh loaves inside, and worked his way from Hartland to Turnpike Gate. Here we assembled to buy a ration of bread. Milk arrived in the same manner; the Symons family delivered at that time and brought churns on a cart from Burnstone farm. Fifteen inches of snow covered the street, but a path was cleared, people are at their best in emergencies, and we were grateful.

1955 and 1969 gave a fair covering of snow. We get at least one day each year, but usually it soon thaws. Not so in 1962-63 though. Great problems arose when, after several weeks of snow, the water pipes seized up, even under the cobbles. School had long been closed – it felt like the Arctic up there! We were lucky. Our one tap gave us water, and we could supply eleven cottages as well as delivering to the older folk. Frozen rain seemed the last straw! No-one could stand on the cobbles, and I clearly remember our postman sitting on his mail-bag and careering down the street! We used old socks over our shoes and boots, and by holding onto a wall, we could just crawl up, or down.

To see the village enveloped in snow is a sight to take one's breath away, it is so lovely. The wrought iron street lamps cast an eerie light, and when lights shine out of the cottage windows, one can imagine oneself in Austria.

"Clovelie"

"The King has a manor called Clovelie, which Britric held on the day on which King Edward was alive and dead. It rendered geld for three hides. These can be ploughed by twelve ploughs. Of them – the King has one hide and five ploughs in demesne. The villeins have two hides and seven ploughs. There the King has 16 villeins, 11 bordars and 10 serfs. 45 head of cattle, 15 swine, 100 sheep and 18 goats. 40 acres of wood, 30 acres of meadow and of pasture – 1 leuga in length and half a leuga in breadth. This manor renders 12 pounds by tale. Goscelm holds this manor to ferm and it rendered 6 pounds when he received it".
(Devonshire Domesday & Geld Inquest).

Thus reads the Domesday description of Clovelly in 1083-86.
"A 'villein' was a farmer. He held land in return for week-work on the lord's land and certain dues. Villeins were the most important class of tenant. Each held about 30 acres – scattered in strips of one or half an acre. His family had to work on the Home Farm, to provide two or more oxen for the manor plough-team. They could not leave the parish, allow their daughter to marry or their son to leave to become a monk or priest, without the lord's permission.

A 'birdar' was a second grade of citizen; a cottager who also worked for the lord, but held no farm-land, only his 'toft' – garden. The bordars lived in boarded or wooden huts. They did not have to supply oxen for the plough-team, but had to pay dues. These would be part of the price of a beast when selling, a fee for corn ground at the mill, and a gift of eggs and hens at Yule and Easter.

A 'cottar' was even lower than a bordar. He and his family were bound to do domestic work at the manor house and to supply food for the lord's table. Similar to our farm-labourer but not having the same freedom.

A 'serf' was almost a slave. They mingled with the cottars and eventually became cottars".
(Living in Medieval England. R.J. Unstead).

Clovelly, or Clovelie is recorded as having 16 villeins, 11 bordars, and 10 serfs. We can assume that the 16 villeins, and 11 bordars each had a wife, making 54 persons, and at least one child per family = 81, plus 10 unmarried serfs = 91 people. We do not know how many lived in the manor house.

"Demesne – Lord's land or home farm
Hide – 120 acres
Geld – Land tax the first system of national taxation to appear in Western Europe
A Furlong – Furrow in length. As far as a plough-team could plough without resting
Plough-team – 8 oxen
Waste – Not yet cultivated
Hay meadows – Lammas land

The Cary crest.

Tithe – One-tenth of the corn crop } paid to the church
1 in 10 new-born animal }
Wood penny – Paid for the right to collect wood in the forest.
There were many dues to be paid to the lord; – when a villein dies; to welcome a new lord; when a daughter married; and when a man took over a new holding". Perhaps we should rejoice over our freedom!
(Living in Medieval England. R.J. Unstead)

Manor and Owners

"The manor, such as it was, passed to William Rufus, who gave the Gloucester properties to Robert, son of Hamon. After his death in 1107, his daughter Matilda's husband, (son of King Henry I), was created Earl and Clovelie remained one of the Gloucester manors until 1346.
It was occupied by the Giffard family from 1242-1298, (or 1303).
They were connected in some way with Weare Giffard.
Sir Matther Giffard died in 1303 leaving two daughters, one of whom married John de Stanton and he is recorded as Lord of the Manor between 1316 and 1324. The manor advowson was divided. It now becomes vague and difffficult to work out. Two families are mentioned and in 1342 the name of Robert de Maundeville is quoted as Lord. At some time between 1346 and 1387, Clovelly became the property of Sir William Cary of St. Giles in the hundred of Torrington. According to one account – he purchased it, and to another, that he married a Thomasine Boson to whom it had passed from the de Stauntons".
(Miss Drakes Note, 1940's).

A notable figure – Mrs Christine Hamlyn outside Clovelly Court with her coachman, Mr. Arnold.

William Cary died in 1396/7 unmarried and so his estates passed to Robert, a nephew. Eleven more Cary owners followed, of which George was the most notable.

"George Cary. DD. Dean of Exeter. Born Clovelly 1611. Baptised 18th July. Was a scholar at Exeter where his father resided. In 1625 he was sent to Queen's College, Oxford. Degree of Arts 1628. Thence to Exeter College. Took holy orders and was presented to the living of Clovelly by his father – Patron – 1639. A constant preacher and pastor for many years. Doctor of Divinity. Refused many preferments. Became Dean of Exeter in September 1663. Lived and died at Shoebrook, Nr. Kirton (Crediton) aged 69". (Prince's Worthies of Devon 1810).

A certain John Cary was created Bishop but never sat on the episcopal throne. He was taken ill in Florence on the way to England, died, and is entombed there. Several owners followed Robert Cary. From 1397 to 1724, it was usually a Cary who ruled from the manor, although every owner did not actually reside there, Cockington (at nearby Abbotsham) also being a Cary mansion.

The last member of the Cary family, Elizabeth, married Robert Barber of Ashmore, Dorset. It would appear that they sold the estate after three hundred years of ownership. The name of the next lord of the manor is "Hamlyn". One branch of this family resided at Marshfield, in the parish of Woolfardisworthy (Woolsery), and another, formerly called "Hammett" at Kennerland, within Clovelly parish.

Zachary of Kennerland succeeded to the Marshfield property on his father's death in 1708. He purchased the Clovelly estate c. 1730, and bequeathed everything to his great-nephew, James Hammett in 1746. James received the property after Zachary died in 1758. He took the Hamlyn name, and married a Williams from a wealthy family in Edwinsford, Carmarthen. The Williams title was added, and the Hamlyn-Williams name continued for several years. In 1824, Susan and Henry Fane inherited Clovelly, and changed their name to Hamlyn-Fane. Their son ruled from 1850-1884, and he was succeeded by his sister, Christine Louise Hamlyn-Fane. So – from Zachary down to Christine, almost two hundred years!

Christine Hamlyn was a most notable owner. She married Frederick Gosling in 1889, and persuaded him to change his name to Hamlyn. She was a fantastic person, a great Christian and friend to everyone. She entertained all sorts and conditions of men (and women). Several bishops and titled people visited

Clovelly in her day. Her staff were loyal, and her tenants loved her. She set such an example. At her death, the whole village mourned, and there were plenty of men to watch over her coffin throughout the night. She loved and cared for her tenants for fifty-two years.

Clovelly passed to her niece, The Hon Mrs B.C. Asquith, and she arranged for a photograph, (taken by my father), to be presented to every tenant. Under it were these words:

"I dwell among mine own people".

The manor was made into a Company in 1929, and the estate is now administered by the Hon John Rous.

We have no idea how the house looked originally. The Cary's built in 1681 and most of this was burnt in 1789. 1790 saw a new building by the Hamlyn's but 1944 saw another fire, with the same wing of the first house surviving both fires!

Clovelly Court – the original wing, survivor of both fires, is on the left.

"I dwell among mine own people".

Paddle steamers from Ilfracombe.

Campbell's steamers cruise around infrequently, but hardly ever land passengers now. Between the wars it was different when hundreds landed, climbed up the street, and hired a carriage and pair to drive through the Hobby. Appetites must have developed after their trip. as the tea-houses were soon filled. Almost every cottage catered for hungry tourists with home-made scones, jam and cream, yeast buns and seedy cake (caraway) usually served for a few pence. We only have one cottage serving food now, but Devon delicacies are generally available. When it was time for the steamer to leave for Ilfracombe or South Wales, short blasts would be sounded on it's siren, and a rush would be made for the harbour and waiting boats. An old photograph shows women wearing skirts which reached their ankles; I fear that problems would have arisen when embarking and disembarking!

I have collected some old shots of the village, and can see pretty well how it looked, but cannot say the same for Higher Clovelly; even sketches are few. We know that Mrs Hamlyn restored several old cottages and farms. We must assume that the thirteen farms, (listed later), needed restoring at some time.

The initials 'CH' with the date cut into the new plaster of many of the cottages refer to Christine Hamlyn who continued her parent's work of restoration, as a result of which some people think Clovelly is younger than it is and the date is the age of the cottage. A few cob cottages are intact, unrestored. Nearly all have some walls of cob, often at the rear; warm red earth and hundreds of years old! Every cottage interior is different from it's neighbour. Stairs are steep and narrow, winding up to tiny attic rooms. Ceilings can be low, not built for tall folk, and windows vary from mini-diamond lattice to strong, wooden-framed sashes – sometimes the cord will snap with disastrous results!

Every cottage is a few inches lower or higher than it's neighbour. This is fine until a chimney lower down the street decides to smoke, and then smuts fly up and smother the lot of us! (How I wish we had a sketch of the older buildings, with their huge chimneys planted in the centre). Fishing families were the original tenants, and no-one could afford a high rent in those days. Sanitation left much to be desired – a shed in the garden sufficed, and in a few instances still does! As one local put it recently: "They was dry closets and us had the best rhubarb in Clovelly!"

1936 – oil lamps soon to be a thing of the past as electricity cables are laid.

1953 – mains water comes to Clovelly.

Wells supplied our water, and how pure it was! A mains supply arrived in 1953, and our beloved wells were sealed off, as was the old reservoir. Sometimes, in heavy rain, the wells will overflow and flood the cellars, where most of them are sited.

Nos. 97, 98 and 99 on the right—No. 99 is now part of the New Inn.

It is very thrilling to find so much cob-walling. We cannot say the exact date of the structures, but cob was widely used in the 1500's. To the red soil was added a portion of straw, (still to be seen on one cottage), or cowhair, and a little water to bind it together. In some walls, we can see small rough stones mixed in with the mud. Usually, a stout cobbled wall up to four feet high forms a foundation wall below. Most of the unrestored cottages contain at least one solid "red-wall" and several are entirely of cob, almost two-thirds of the total of 75 cottages. One complete cob building, No 76, is tucked away in a side turning. It is quite unique – two small windows are deeply set in the thick walls, 20″ x 20″ and 24″ x 24″ – just a sheet of glass. The view over the bay is delightful.

Near this cottage stands a larger dwelling, No 77. Only part of the wall facing us contains cob. High up is a square wooden door, and the only approach is by a ladder! Inside is a beautiful carved plaster ceiling, said to be 600 years old. The rest of the house was restored in 1918, but has retained a mellow atmosphere.

In the High Street, opposite the front door of No 77, a tall cottage, No 26, built entirely of cob, where some walls are three feet thick. The tenant told me that inside it is never too warm in summer, and always comfortable in winter. What more could we ask of a cottage?

No 74, next to the doctor's surgery, is quite unspoilt. All walls are of cob, and old beams support the roof over one of the smallest kitchens imaginable.

North Hill.

The North Hill turning closeby is very steep, and leads up past old cottages to the Peace Park or Little Field, with it's seats and monumental cross.

At the bottom of North Hill, look at the three cottages leading away to the right. All are unrestored, – thick cob walls are visible behind, third along, now re-roofed – 1984.

Opposite the Post Office is No 80, cob cottage through and through. A 'bun' oven, with another older one surrounding it, was uncovered in 1974. Bread was baked inside this square cavity, built into the right-hand side of the fireplace, which was of stone. A huge fire in the middle was never allowed to go out, and often an iron pot was suspended from a chain. Stews and suchlike would be cooked in this way.

Three doors up the street on the right, is No 20, a minute cottage of one staircase, with one up and one down on each side. Two old ladies once dwelt here, using the same set of stairs. We hope they got on well!

Up four doors to No 16, a larger house and once owned by a wealthy person. There are two staircases and four levels, including a cellar, hardly changed over the centuries. There are not many abodes here which can boast four levels. The exception is the Post Office and store, which has five or six, and although restoration was carried out in 1904, much of this irregularly shaped dwelling is as before.

No 97, the cafe, has four levels but was rebuilt in 1888, as was No 98 next door. No 99 is now part of the New Inn.

Nos. 19, 20 and 21, High Street.

The New Inn sign hung on the left-hand side looking down the street, as this was the main part of the inn until about 1914. Above the sign stood two small wooden figures, a soldier and a sailor. Their arms moved backwards and forwards when the east wind blew. Into the left-hand corner of the building was fitted the bar, quite small, but snug, and coloured glass ornaments decorated the window-ledge. To the right of the steps lay the smoking-room, taproom and kitchen. Boxes of plants were displayed outside on the verandah.

In days of old, the hotel or inn must have been charming. A well-satisfied customer writes: "The dining-room was beautifully furnished, blue and white willow pattern plates lined the walls, and brass and copper warming-pans gleamed in the firelight. The food was delicious, all locally produced, and it soon revived us after our long journey." Three tiny cottages in Back Lane were swallowed up in the restoration carried out in 1913-14, and now form the bar. This is opposite the Methodist Chapel. Stables occupied the higher part until 1889.

Changing sides—The New Inn on the left.

Murray's Handbook of Devon and Cornwall, 1859, says:

"Here the traveller should rest a day at the little inn, which will entertain him with great hospitality. If it happens to be the autumn, he may regale at breakfast upon herrings which have been captured overnight. For Clovelly is famed for it's fishery and every evening about sunset, the boats may be observed leaving the shore to 'drive' for herrings or mackerel. In thick weather (i.e. favourable), a Clovelly boat has captured as many as 9,000 herrings at a haul, selling at 18/- to 25/- for a maise which consists of 612 fish."

Nostalgic thoughts, indeed!

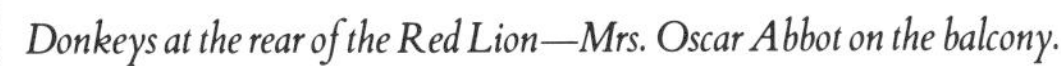
Donkeys at the rear of the Red Lion—Mrs. Oscar Abbot on the balcony.

We find a pleasing reference to the Red Lion, too.

"The Red Lion is an old house, charming turnings and lots of steps and dark passages. The supper was delicious. Fried chicken, green peas and new potatoes, raspberries and clotted cream. Great vases of flowers are on the tables. They put you to bed with candles, you sleep to the sound of the tide, and wake up to the most glorious view of the bay and shore, and feel glad to be alive."

The Red Lion is really a collection of cottages, hence the "turnings, steps and dark passages." We know that Nos 50, 51 and 52 are part of it, and someone told me that as many as six cottages were joined up!

The Red Lion, showing once a collection of cottages.

The old saw pit is on the right: Crazy Kate's is on the left of the row of cottages and the Waterhouse (boat building shed) is beyond.

Some buildings come to mind which have never been dwellings. Mr James Whitefield was a Clovelly man, and once told me much about the quay area.

"The sand-house, opposite the limekiln, housed sand which had been dredged from a site near the waterfall. It was used throughout the estate for building purposes until 1910. Donkeys were used to transport it to the top. Before sand was stored, the lower part served as a blacksmith's shop. Old Burman was the smith and lived over. The entrance can still be seen on the right."

"Boats were built and repaired by my father, another Jim Whitefield, in the cellar next door, (facing us as we come down the street.) He finished in 1925. John Mills built boats in this cellar before my father. A cellar behind the Red Lion was owned and used by Robert Hodge for boat-building. In the 1860's, or so, there was a boat-house up the beach, towards Bucks."

"The saw-pit" was just below the limekiln. Here, wood was sawn into planks by two men, who used a huge saw, and struggled to push their way through until a large pile of planks lay on the beach, and the pit beneath was full of sawdust."

Cottages number from 1 to 108a in the village, continue through Wrinkleberry, up on the left-hand side and down on the right-hand side of Slerra, ending at the bottom with 155. 68 cottages are occupied in the village. Cottage rents are paid on quarter days to the Clovelly Estate Company, and until 1976 rates and water rates were very low. Lady Day March 25; Midsummer June 24; Michaelmas Sept 29; Xmas Dec 25.

Several years ago, a preservation order was placed on the cottages. Now, a conservation plan has been passed. Add on the fact the Mrs Hamlyn firmly controlled any alterations or developments, and we can thank God that Clovelly is , and has been, so protected.

Lime was always used to sweeten the fronts of the cottages in springtime. 2/6d would purchase enough to do this and leave a little over for the backyards so lightening the kitchens, which were usually at the back. The effect was one of startling brilliance. The cobbled street was spotless, – again, everyone took a pride in their domain. We saw less litter years ago, too.

About sixty years ago purchases could be made at a number of cottages;

No 12 – Velvet-lined trinket boxes and postcards.
A sign outside with "Views of the neighbourhood."
Nos 13-14 – "Good beds" on sign outside.
No 99 – Walking sticks, tall crooked sticks, baskets.
No 98 – Jewell's tea and coffee rooms.
No 19 – One could buy a reel of cotton and a knot of tape from old Vic Pengelly.
No 74 – Pengelly's Refreshment Room.

Mary Ann Smale kept a sweet shop. We could get 16 aniseed balls for 1d, and scented alphabet letters in a tiny v-shaped bag.

No 20 – Sold tea.

(There was a tiny shop in the garden of No 96. Mr Jim Whitfield was taken inside it 84 years ago. Soon after, it was pulled down.

The dead-house, or mortuary, was constructed in 1898, the gift of Mr Hamlyn. This building is next to the old coastguard hut at the foot of the turnpike road, behind the Red Lion, where a land-rover now carries passengers who cannot walk up the main street.

The coastguard hut was next to the mortuary, behind the Red Lion. A fire-place still exists at one end. There is an unbroken view from here, and the coastguards on duty would patrol to Mouth Mill, either along the beach or over the park.

A flag belonging to the Rechabites flew from a pole fixed on the Look-out, and that of the Shipwrecked Mariners from a staff outside No 105, High Street.

Grain was shipped over to Wales in exchange for coal, – money was almost unheard of. One cellar still shows a few grains, but there were at least three granaries in 1815.

No 108a stands on the site of old stables. Horses and carts used to come down as far as the Fountain. The animals would rest here, and fresh horses take their place. Eventually a new block was built in 1889, mainly for the use of the New Inn, at the far end of the lower car park. These stables are now used for donkeys and an old drinking trough stands outside. At the garage end is a room used in the early 1900's for gay evenings singing and dancing. One chap would "dance the broomstick", a lcoal version of Scottish dancing.

From time to time, a whist drive or film show is held there and recently, the British Legion, have given the building a face-lift and formed a "Social Club."

The two chapels have never been living quarters, although St Peter's was used in wartime for children's classes. The first Youth Club, organised by the Rev A Chandler, held meetings there; as did Girl Guides and Brownies, started during his seven years here.

The Methodist Chapel has only been used for services. Mr "Fred" was caretaker, and would speak of when the chapel was full to the door, and the voices were so strong the roof almost took off! He died in 1978.

Anniversary services are held in all the chapels in May on the nearest Sunday to Whit Sunday. Children would usually bring a posy, which was given to someone sick. The regular attenders would receive a book as a reward. A memorial to Capt Charles Bate will be found on the end wall. He was of an old Clovelly family, now extinct. The words "My house is the house of prayer" are written over the preacher's desk.

Taken from the Hobby – on the right are the stables used by the New Inn.

Population – Occupation – Habitation

I think this heading will cover all I can say about any or all of the titles. They are completely woven into each other.

We have population figures from 1801 to the 1970's.

1801 = 714	1891 = 741
1841 = 990	1901 = 621
1851 = 937	1931 = 528
1861 = 825	1961 = 445
1881 = 787	1976 = 390

(158 village. 232 Hr Clovelly = 299 adults, 91 children.)

The electoral roll of October 1975 is misleading, now. Several people mentioned have died, moved, or are not permanent residents in the parish now.

From 1841 there is movement away from Clovelly, maybe only to the next village. Fishing was growing less profitable, and farm workers' pay was no more than a pittance.

In 1815, we find a list of house-holders who actually owned their dwellings, or had them on life-leases, but as the last member of a family died, the property was sold to the landlord. Very often, the building was crumbling and much money would be needed to restore it. (From Mrs Hamlyn's records.)

Mrs Percy Jones was a native of Clovelly. Before she died in January 1972, she told me so much about the village. One or two facts are worth remembering. "Fifty children lived below the Look-out." (As there are only 17 cottages, each family must have been quite large.) She quoted some old Clovelly names, too, – "Jewell, Cruse, Whitefield, Dunn, Pengelly, Howard, Headon, Moss, Shackson, Burnard, Beer, Prince, Badcock, Bate, Elliot, Hortop." "Complete families would walk across the park on a Sunday afternoon. and always attend church or chapel, usually in the evening." What a happy village, – certainly a God-fearing community!

Beer Hcuses. There were several beer-houses in Clovelly, at least one in Higher Clovelly at 115 or 116 Slerra, one at 58 The Quay; three behind the Red Lion; Cliff Cottage had one before it was pulled down; a cottage below the doctor's surgery, No 104; and No 10 – this was probably in the cellar. The New Inn was a beer-house until a full licence was granted. A Mr Ebsworthy ran the beer house in what is now No 58 The Quay. All the gardens on the right side looking down the street were in the control of this Mr Ebsworthy. Those on the left came under the New Inn.

In Mrs Hamlyn's records (1815), we read that "Mr Barrow kept the smith's shop for a term of fourteen years from 1810." (This is now the old sand-house down at the quay.) "Next door – Capt Hockin keeps a granary."

White's Directory of 1850 gives a little information:-

"Some residents in the parish of Clovelly.
Sir J H Williams of Clovelly Court.
Rev Z H Drake – The Rectory.
H Dalton – Curate.
James Finch – Beer cellar.
W Heard – Grocer and draper.
Hockington – Court garden.
Parsons – Tailor.
Ann Whitefield – Grocer and draper.
Whitefield – New Inn.
Vine Westlake – Red Lion.
Grills
Bierman
Nichols } *We know that three shoemakers lived in No. 42, 47 and 64).*
There are 2 granaries. (In cellars near the harbour.)
John Dannell is postmaster, parish clerk and schoolmaster.
Catherine Jewell is a shopkeeper."
(This was my great-grandmother.)
1889 Living is £244.
C H Fane is lady of the manor.
Sub-soil is clay and rock.
Chief crops – oats and wheat.
3,502 acres. Rateable value is £2,309.
Pop. in 1881 = 787.
Parish clerk is Richard Parsons. Rev Harrison – Rector.
R G Cooke is surgeon and also to the Coast Guards.
John Jewell – Master mariner.
Mrs Emma Whitefield – Fancy dealer.
John Mill – Boat-builder.
Berriman at New Inn.
Wm Moss – Smack owner and coal director.
Carrier is Samuel Jewell, helped by Wm Jeffrey.
Bideford – Tuesdays, Thursdays and Saturdays.
Lifeboat Station – Beach – Richard Headon (Capt.)
Coastguard Station – Frederick C Ashby. 1 Officer, 6 men.
Insurance agent for West of England – J H Seldon.
Board School opened in 1872 for 150 children.
Av. attendance is 110.
J Hobbs Seldon – master.
William Tucker Howard is postmaster.
Letters are received from Bideford at 9.25 a.m. and dispatched at 4.30 p.m. 3.30 on Sundays."

The name of 'Braund' does not appear until the first member of this clan, Albert, rowed down from Bucks, his wife and their worldy goods in the small boat with him. They settled here and brought up a large family. Three more members followed suit, Alfred, Herbert and Harold. They married local girls, and all but Albert lived below "The Look-out," or "The Hill." This name, Braund, lives on, as do Shackson, Dunn and Headon.

Let me introduce some of the Clovelly folk who talked with me; Mrs F Cruse, Mrs M E Abbott, Mr & Mrs William Braund, Mrs L Edwards, Mr J Whitefield, Mr G Lamey, Mr Fred Robbins, Mr & Mrs Shackson, and Mr Tom Cruse. Some of their words are set down as spoken. Their stories are all true and I am so grateful for the many happy hours spent in their company.

The Cruses lived at No 75 – "Star Cottage" – for over 100 years, the longest tenants, (our family coming second, since 1902 to the present day.) A Cruse looked after "The Old Lodge." This was the entrance to The Hobby, and is now called "London Lodge."

Five generations back, a Cruse planted the first roots of "London Pride" near the second bridge in The Hobby. Their grandfather clock moved down to No 75, and was nailed to the wall during their long tenancy.

Charles Kingsley's cot lay in their lobster-pot shed until a few years ago. It was worm-eaten and so was burnt – Tom Cruse sadly regrets it now. Old Mrs Cruse had moved with the Kingsley family as nursemaid in the 1830's, and stayed on to marry. Mrs Flora Cruse died in 1980.

The names of Moss and Burnard are no more. The last ex-Moss was Mrs Abbott, who died in 1982. Her stories of long ago would grip the imagination. Oscar was her husband, and together they could cover life in Clovelly back to the early 1900's.

Moss and Cruse alternated in the ownership of a coal-boat, the "Lucy." She travelled to and fro from South Wales, and would arrive in the harbour bearing 60 tons of coal. She tied up at the "coal-slip" part of the pier. A plank was laid from her deck to the quay, a wheel-barrow would be filled, (approx 1 cwt) and someone would wheel it along to the cellars beneath the Red Lion. If the coal was purchased and collected, the price was 10d per cwt. If a donkey struggled up the street with a load on either side, (wooden box-panniers rested on the back of the donkey), the cost rose to 1/- per cwt. For 200 years, this was the way coal came to Clovelly. The practice ended in 1927 when the cellars were incorporated into the Red Lion, and now form the bar.

Behind the Red Lion—the end of the Turnpike Road.

We know that in 1800 coal was being landed at Mouth Mill for the use of the manor house. Donkeys again carried it away. A narrow gut or gulley allowed a small ship to move in and land the coal.

A family named Beer once lived in Mouth Mill cottage. One dark February night, a swarthy sailor knocked on the door and asked to speak with "the missus." A youth told him that his mother was in bed with a new-born baby. The stranger said, "What will you call him?" The boy answered, "We already have seven, sir, and have used up all the names." "Call it 'Emmanuel' after me", the man stated, and that was how Emmanuel Beer got his name! His daughter, Evelyn was married to our last lifeboat coxswain, William Braund, and they lived near the harbour. Their kitchen was "on the beach", and is converted from a cellar. This cottage has been greatly restored. William's father was also coxswain, (1929-32). His sister, Mary was married to George Lamey, coxswain from 1935-55, and he still collected money for lifeboat work – until too ill to stand. In one year he reached his target of collecting £1,000, and gained yet another award to display in his cottage.

"The Hamlyns employed some local men to keep the estate in good repair. Buildings all over the parish, along with the Hobby woods, paths, hedges and ditches, gave work for many months. There was no-one unemployed in those days; everyone did a day's work for a day's pay.

The fishermens' wives filled their time by making new nets of cotton. Fish earnings were pretty small, – so was new cotton, though." So says Mr Jim Whitefield.

Trawling gear was made by the men. He also named eight trawlers which worked here until 1920 or so. These included the three Braund boats, plus the *Flying Fish* (Jeffrey), *Victory* (Pengelly), *Ware* (S Headon), *Ebenezer* (R Braund of Bucks), and *Owen Glendower* (T Pengelly). The *Ebenezer* was registered in Bideford in 1845 by Reuben Braund of Buckish, Weight 18 ton. (From the Alphabetical List of Maritime Directories, in the keeping of Mr G Lamey).

George Lamey told of Clovelly most beautifully. Although over 80, he remembers details vividly. Appledore was his birthplace, the sixth generation of Lamey. As a small boy, he would sit with Coxswain Smallridge of Appledore lifeboat. All his cousins were lifeboat-men, and the sea has continued to be his calling. He joined a ship in 1914, but it caught fire. Finding another, which he loved, disaster came again, for they were torpedoed near Malta. Nothing daunted, he was sent to Antwerp, where he met Brigadier-General Arthur Asquith, and served a period with him.

In 1918, he came to Clovelly to stay with his aunt at "Rat's Castle." On looking out of the window, he spotted the local post-girl, Mary Braund, and decided that she was the girl for him! They married in 1921. Mr Caird, the Estate Agent, offered him a job, parking cars. He later worked on the estate.

Sad to report, the people of Clovelly were unkind to him at first. Reason? He was from Appledore, one of Clovelly's rivals! Great jealousy existed between villages then, and we recalled the old saying together:-

"Clovelly row-dogs,
Peppercombe brags,
But little Bucks nanny-goats
Will tear 'em all to rags."

However, he joined the Clovelly lifeboat, and served under Coxswain T Pengelly, who respected him for his knowledge of the sea. Then followed a spell with his father-in-law, Coxswain

The Cruse family making lobster pots from withies.

Alfred Braund. Finally, he became Coxswain, and served from 1935-55. He has received several acknowledgements for daring rescue work, including a Bronze Medal and two vellums. I think the most rewarding experience was remembered in August 1975. Herr Rudolph Graff returned to say 'Thank you' to him and his crew for saving his life in August 1942. The German 'plane had come down, and the three men were in a dinghy off Hartland Point. When the lifeboat arrived, the little craft was leaking badly, and to make things more dramatic, the lifeboat engine exploded! Sails were used for the return journey, and I think the RAF helped out with a launch to tow the boat in. Herr Graff brought photos of himself then and now, and a beer stein for each surviving crew member, of which there were four.

George fished with the Cruse family, Dick and his father, Tom, and so gained much of the information given to me. Old Tom and his sons made their lobster-pots in a shed near their cottage. Withies (willows), were needed, and these they grew in a woody garden. Times were hard then and families larger – fish often being their main subsistance.

Harriet Jewell and Aunt Maria knitting socks.

A rope-walk existed on the higher side of the Stream, (the old river from the High Street), which runs through the woods down to the sea. Here local men spent many hours weaving strong ropes, beginning by No 108a and ending at the top of the old rubbish dump, which was closed in 1976. Rope-making occurred in most fishing ports and continued until the 1900's.

I was delighted to hear him describe the run of the old stream, and it was just as I have stated. He crawled up through the culvert many years ago. An interesting area lay near the beginning of the stream, by No 106. Under the garden of No 77 is the arch where a man called "Chesil" once hid, to avoid the press gang. His wife fed him there, and called "Ducky-ducky" in the pretence of feeding ducks. (This story has been passed down through many old Clovelly families.)

Recently I spent an afternoon with Mr Fred Robins who is the oldest man in Clovelly. He lives at Wrinkleberry, in the house in which he was born 83 years ago. His father too was "Fred" and his grandfather Henry was carried into the house when seven weeks old to be brought up by an aunt as his mother had died in childbirth. This makes the Robins family the longest tenants in the parish.

He told me that his mother was a servant at the Court with Mrs Hamlyn and all the staff were given a new uniform to wear when Christine married Mr Gosling. There were great celebrations.

I asked him what happened on rent days when he was young. "Oh us had a free dinner of venison pie, a glass of beer and cigarettes to smoke."

Some more information – "There was Jewells living in every cottage in Wrinkleberry about 1800 and there's 5 cottages."

And again – "Your grandfather used to teach me in Sunday School – he was a good man and I liked to see him painting in the street." A funny rhyme which someone used to sing when he had tanked up with beer at the New Inn.

"When I die – don't bury me at all
Just pickle my bones in alcohol
A bottle of beer at my head and feet
And then I'm sure my bones will keep."

(Fred is a keen gardener still).

I should like to tell you about someone who lived amongst us for many years – Miss Harriet Jewell. Always known as "Harty", she grew up in the village along with her many brothers and sisters. For a number of years she was away "in service", returning home to nurse her ailing mother and sister. After their deaths, her aged Aunt Maria moved into No 106, and received the same loving care from Harty, who was then in her 80's.

Mary Heywood, then over 90, could hardly move or see, and so sat many hours by the fire, knitting socks for the Church of England Children's Society. Together, they made dozens of pairs, which my mother, as local secretary, passed on to the various Homes.

Harty also helped raise money for the lifeboats, and she received a Silver Medal for her devotion to this cause.

Her father was the local carrier for many years, and the red plush-covered chair in church was given in his memory.

Harty never varied her way of life, always ready to support any good cause, but church was her first love. When she could no longer climb the hill, she worshipped in St Peter's. Truly, she was a saint and greatly missed.

At least three generations of Shacksons have lived in Clovelly. The oldest member "Mr Fred" as we called him, told me where to find some of the old wells.

"There's one in the cafe, Mrs Friend's place, in the kitchen; in the cellar of No 10; No 15 has got one, that's in the cellar, too; underneath the Post office is one, and that one overflows sometimes. Miss Webb has got one, and Mr Butcher, – his was two houses, but one is almost gone now, though. There was a hatch-door, like a stable, do you know? Well, inside was a pump for getting up the water. 'Twas good water, too."

He told me the story of No 11, The White Cottage.

"A Captain and Mrs Mills lived there, up to the middle 1890's. He spent a lot of time at sea and drank too much liquor. His poor wife became desperate and could stand no more. One day, she left the cottage, bowed three times to no-one in particular, and threw herself off a cliff first removing her bonnet."

The cottage was sold to Mrs Hamlyn for £25, and restored. The attic roof is held up by three sets of beams, all slightly curved, and said to have come from an old ship. The original cob main wall remains.

One more cottage must be mentioned, Providence House or No 86. This is an old structure with several floor levels, making life difficult. A high wall curves up by the first flight of stairs, cob, of course. The top set is steep and dangerous, and it is not possible to move furniture up. I suppose it has only been used for storage. Both up and down-stairs the floor levels vary, just as though two cottages had been joined. The rear has not survived as it was. A long room stretched out from where the kitchen now is. An old photo shows steps going up to the next cottage, and two bedrooms were joined in. No-one knows why it was changed, as it is now rather a hotch-potch.

Immediately opposite is a small garden. This space once contained a tiny cottage which was a shop.

A garden in North Hill is the site of No 28, another tiny dwelling. The other two missing numbers, 29 and 30, were sited above No 31 on a steep ridge, both small and of cob.

Lastly, No 5, which stood in a patch off the lane, or Steepways, had become derelict. A pile of debris and local rubbish lay there for forty years, until I cleared it and made a garden in ten days, now called "The Instant Garden."

Mount Pleasant Row and No. 5—now "my instant garden".

A list of cottages in the order we find them may help the reader to "tour the village."

Mount Pleasant is on our left coming down the lane, about 100 yards from the lower car park.

No. 1. Much restored cottage, far end of row.
2. Cob wall at rear.
3/4. Completely restored 1899. Formerly old Reading Room. Branch of National Westminster Bank (monthly) until 1975.
5. Pulled down. Now "Instant Garden" 1971.

The Fountain – Memorial to Queen Victoria.
6/7. Restored 1925. Cob at rear.
8. Outer walls cob.

High Street. (Left-hand side going down.)
9. "Kingsley Cottage." Cob through and through.
10. Cob all through. (Well.) Old beer-house.
11. "White Cottage." Restored 1902. (and again in 1984).

New Inn Annexe. Restored 1918. Now only bedrooms.
12. Restored 1921. Once covered in wall geranium, fuchsias and species fuchsia – "Thalia."
14. Partly restored 1921. Some cob at rear.
15. Restored 1896. (Well.)
16. Large and unrestored.
17/18. Two into one 1918. Cob rear and end.
19. Restored 1909. Cob rear and end, could have joined No 18.
20. Original. (Showing straw). Restored.
21. Built 1865 for local doctor. Inside re-made 1912.
22. Partly restored, 1904. Cob at rear.
23. Post Office and Store. Partly restored 1904. (Well). Cob at rear.
24/25. Two into one. Cob at rear.
26. Entirely of cob – 3 feet thick in parts.

North Hill. (Left-hand side going up.)
27. Cob end and back, at least.
28. Gone. Now tiny garden.

North Hill. (Opposite side, coming down.)
29. Gone.
30. Cob. Very tiny.
31. } Partly restored. Cob rear.
32. }

At bottom of North Hill, turn left.
33. Cob.
34. Cob. Practically unchanged.
35. Practically unchanged inside reroofed.
36.
37. Rebuilt 1910. Oberammergau carving over door.
38. Gone.
39. Gone. Old Bill Burman's cottage, fallen off cliff.

Around the corner at "Back Side" – note the tea garden on the cliff edge before its collapse.

Mount Pleasant Cottages—Reading Room and National Provincial Bank and Jack Prince.

Rose Cottage, Roland Hortop and donkey.

Retrace steps and turn left to "Look-out" or "The Hill."

40. Hardly changed in centuries. A delightful roof.
41. Has some cob.

On our left going down.

42. Cellar. Some cob. Old shoemaker's cottage.
43. "Rose Cottage." Rebuilt 1952.
44. Almost unchanged. One of the oldest.

We walk under "The Bow" or "Temple Bar."

45/46. Outer as before, ancient. Inside re-made in 1973.
47. Cellar. (Old shoemaker.)

A few more steps to "Rats' Castle" on our left.

48. Some cob.
Old Blacksmith's and sand-house, (left), Cellar ahead.
Limekiln on right.

We reach the bottom of the High Street.

49. Next to the Red Lion.
50/52. Woven into the hotel, hence many passages, tiny rooms and endless steps.

Through the gatehouse or arch, we see ahead the granary cellar and old coastguard hut which was used before the new building in the higher car park. (A fireplace remains.)

Return and stroll along towards Crazy Kate's cottage and it's neighbour.

53. "Crazy Kate's." The oldest cottage in Clovelly.
54. Inside is much as it was. Both were re-roofed and bathroom built on.

A block of three cottages stand on the wharf in front, – Fish Street at the back.

55. } Attractive buildings, though not old.
56. } Rebuilt by Mrs Hamlyn.
57. }

Lifeboat house next and former stream outlet.

58. } Old beer-house. "The Jolly Sailor."
59. } All restored by Mrs Hamlyn.
60. }

Up a few steps.

61. Rebuilt after cliff fall. Restored again in 1970's.

Tucked around a corner on our right:-

62/3. Outside is unchanged.
64. Now a cellar. Old shoemaker's.

Continue up steep steps and arrive back at "The Bow."

We climb up to the "Look-out" and turn sharp left to Independent Street.

65. "Cliff Cottage." Rebuilt in 1962. Originally beer-house.
66. Gone. Now vegetable garden.

On the opposite side:-

67. Pulled down. Now small garden.
68. Rebuilt 1929. A little cob.
69/70. Rebuilt 1930.
71/72. Rebuilt 1930. Font found in wall.

Re-trace steps to "Look-out" again and turn left up High Street.

73. Rebuilt 1912. Oberammergau carving. Formerly two cottages, one a beer-house. (Doctor's surgery.)
74. Quite unchanged and charming. Formerly cafe and shop.

Down some steps on the left, with iron handrail.

75. "Star Cottage." Cruse dwelling for over 100 years. Roof re-made in 1930. (Restored recently).

Turn right for:-

76. Original – wonderful. Recently gutted and re-made.

Climb the steps again to High Street, turn left.

77. Restored 1918. Ceiling saved.
78/79. Gift shop. Two into one, though still unusual inside. Several windows blocked to avoid Window Tax.

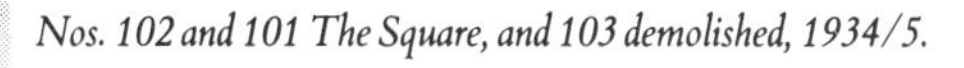
Nos. 102 and 101 The Square, and 103 demolished, 1934/5.

80. Cob. Cloam oven unearthed in 1974.
81. Cob right through.
82. Some cob. There was a passage-way through, before the next block of cottages were rebuilt.
83. Stone. About 120 years old.
84. Stone. About 120 years old.
85. Large cottage made into two dwellings (Well)
85a.
86. Providence House.

Turn left into Providence Row.

87/88. Cob. (Well.) About to be gutted.

St Peter's Chapel here.

89/90. Two made into one 1919. Much cob.
91. Now estate store-room.

Continue up Back Lane to Methodist Chapel on left.
Turn around and face down again.

92/93 Built into New Inn wall and now part of bar. An archway to New Inn rear – cob in this wall.

Moving down again:-

94/95. Two made into one and rebuilt. A mixed-up cottage.
96. Part of this very old cottage is built across the lane.

Along to the left-hand corner and proceed up High Street again.

97. The Cafe. Rebuilt in 1888.
98. Rebuilt 1888.
99. Now part of the New Inn kitchen and dining-room.

Pass the New Inn and turn left round the corner, across to the Square. At the far left:-

100. Restored. Cob at the rear, showing straw.
101. Very much restored.
102. Very much restored.
103. Taken down in 1934/5. Cob. Old penny found in wall.
104. Much original work here. Now two cottages. (Well outside.) Old beer-house.

Return to High Street, turn left.

105. Practically unchanged. Roof re-made 1973/4.
106. Some cob.
107. Cob.
108.

Cob and stone.

108a. Rebuilt in 1963/4. Formerly site of the stables, and we are back at the Fountain!

6, 7 and 8 The Fountain.

The Coach arriving.

Transport

"The roads are painful for man and horse, as they can best witness, who have made trial thereof. Specimens of what the roads formerly were, are yet visible in many places and shew at once that a passage for wheel carriages was not contemplated in their formation. Turnpikes began to be formed about the year 1753."
(Risdon's Survey of Devon c1600.)

A carrier's cart from Clovelly to Bideford was the only form of transport until the motor-car arrived. Two horses pulled the waggon, five people could ride inside, but had to get out and walk up all the hills. The surface was rough, – very dusty in dry weather, and equally nasty when much rain had fallen.

Coaches would come from Ilfracombe, – 35 miles away. In 1896, it was the custom to stay overnight in Barnstaple, and make the rest of the journey to Clovelly or on to Bude, the following day. The guard, or conductor, would sit on a high seat in front of the passengers. When nearing the village, he would play a musical selection on his post-horn, and men would hurry to the top of the cobbles to help passengers alight, and to carry down their luggage. These visitors were mostly from the USA. Horses were changed at the stables if the coach was going on to Bude, and two delightul coaches were on view locally, until the danger from vandals became too great.

Nothing but donkeys and sledges can move on the cobbled street; all vehicles are prohibited. Sledges have been fully described, but the donkeys must have their purpose explained. Gone are the days of sheer cruelty when the poor animals were carrying such heavy loads. Now, they are looked after by Roger and Gwen Balfour, who have been vegetarians for many years, and Sue Green who is also a saddle maker. The animals are treated with love and respect. They brought donkeys to Clovelly. I had purchased three, a baby donkey called "Simon" which Mrs Rous brought home in her car, (he 'cried' all over Christmas, I remember), "Kingsley" (after Charles), and "Eeyore", who so fitted his name that it stuck! Mr Cecil Braund had Peter and Paul, a cousin had "Jenny", and Mrs Rous had "Queenie", "Charlie" and "Chloe."

Donkeys waiting for customers.

The New Inn—on the right, with the sign surmounted by the wooden soldier and sailor.

Wooden panniers are fitted across the backs of "Isaac" and "Daniel" who belong to Sue Green, with soft packing underneath to prevent chafing.

These are used to transport luggage, laundry and refuse from the New Inn up to the lower car park. If Sue thinks the load is too great, she removes some and carries it up herself.

Until recently the Balfours stood near the New Inn with Liza and Ruby for visitors to photograph, but they and five other donkeys are now living in retirement in Cornwall.

Sadly the High Street is now too congested for donkeys to toil up and down giving rides to the children, but Sue's donkey cart does take them for short rides along the hobby drive.

A brave motorist – out of bounds.

Trawlers in the Quay Pool.

Fishing

Fishing, alas, has declined, over-fishing being the chief cause; not only here though. Canadian visitors told the same story recently.

In 1900, around fifty small herring boats would launch out each evening bearing two men, returning at day-break with thousands of shining, slippery fish. Wives and daughters would arrive and help "shake the nets". Herrings would be counted three at a time up to 612 a "meas" and dropped into a mawn – a deep, round basket with two handles then fixed on either side of donkeys. These strong animals would carry their burden up a rugged track known as the Turn-pike, to waiting lorries, which then took the cargo to Bideford. Finally, a train would transport the famous "Clovelly herrings" to London and other counties.

Cod was caught in large quantities too. Tithes of fish were paid to the Rector. The Lord of the manor received his harbour dues in fish, until an insufficient quantity were caught – "the second best pair of soles if more than twenty were caught at a time" -- did not bring forth a great amount of wealth!

> *"In contrast to the pilchard which was caught steadily (on the south coast), from the 14th to the early 19th century, the herring sometimes disappeared for years on end – causing great distress at Clovelly, Ilfracombe and Lynmouth. It was scarce again about 1805. Clovelly had at one time 60 or 70 boats in the herring fishery, but had much declined by the time Lysons wrote (1822) Large quantities were exported."*
>
> *"In 1840 the name of Clovelly is still listed among the chief fishing ports."*
> *(Survey of Devon – Prof. W.G. Hoskins).*

About 1840, trawling for fish began to be important in Clovelly. The harbour was filled with these vessels until the 1920's. There were no motor-engines then, and unless the right sort of wind was blowing, the trawlers were "grounded" inside the harbour. There were fewer stones to cope with in those far off days. Old photos show as many as nine trawlers lying within the quay pool, locally called 'Kay Puul'.

Mr Will Braund told me that his father's boats, the *"J.H.L."*, the *"Chase"* and the *"Teazer"* were the last vessels to work here.

In the record book of Clovelly's harbour master in the 1830's, he writes:

> *"There are now 72 boats in all, 6 largeboats, 50 small boats and in addition, 16 boats are employed in the taking of large fish."*
>
> *The harbour dues –*
> *1814 paid on 6,005 maise of herrings*
> *1822 paid on 495 maise of herrings*
> *1823 paid on 1,680 maise of herrings*
> *1816 31,200 bushels of corn.*
> *In November 1807, herrings sold at 25/- for a maise.*

Herring boats landing their catch – 1930's.

Trawlers in the Quay Pool.

We find similar records alluding to the coming and going of herrings, 1740–46:-

"In the year 1740, God was pleased to send us his blessing of a great fishery among us – after a failure of many years. This through his mercy continued in 1741. In the year 1742, the fish was small and poor, and in less quantities. In this year 1743, but an indifferent fishing. In this year 1744, worse than in the preceding. In this year 1745, still worse. In the year 1746, much worse."

"In those days, many men from surrounding villages congregated in Clovelly for the fishing season, as the following information shows:- There were 46 burials between August 17th, 1742 and May 15th, 1743 – nine months! 28 have already died of smallpox, including a Welsh lad, a stranger, a lad of Northam, a youth from Combe Martin, and a showmaker from Stratton. John Dyer of Tamerton fell over the key in this fishing season. John Robbins, Rector."

(This was copied into an old Church magazine.)

Fishing nets drying on the Top Quay.

The lime kiln and Crazy Kate's cottage on far left.

Kate Lyall, (known as 'Crazy Kate,') died in 1736. She lived in what is reputed to be the oldest cottage in Clovelly. Kate would watch her husband from an upper window as he fished in the bay. One day, he was drowned before her eyes and she became demented. Sad to report, she remained so until her death. The cottage still goes by the name of 'Crazy Kate's and is situated right on the beach. The kitchen was flooded in 1974 during exceptionally high tides. This was formerly a cellar and cobbles formed the floor until they were covered with cement a few years back. It's hard to imagine the sea in a full gale, waves rolling and breaking on the outside of the harbour wall and spume rises high in the air.

A terrible fishing disaster happened in 1821. Sixty herring boats were caught in a gale which sprang up in a few minutes. This account has been taken from the Church magazine of 1911.

"On Oct. 4th 1821, occurred one of the most disastrous storms ever known in Bideford Bay. Thirty-one fishermen perished in it leaving 19 widows and 61 children. A large number of boats and many nets were lost. In that gale, 11 men from Clovelly perished.

Name	*Burial*	*Age*	*Widow's name*	*Family*
Thomas Beer	*Oct. 7*	*45*	*Joanna*	*6*
Wm. Colwill	*,, 8*	*39*	*Mary*	*1*
Jonathan Jewell	*,, 9*	*36*	*Mary*	*5*
Th. White	*,, 11*	*45*	*Grace*	*0*
Wm. Fulford	*,, 11*	*31*	*Elizabeth*	*4*
John Waters	*,, 13*	*37*	*Mary*	*8*
James Branton	*,, 15*	*32*	*Mary*	*3*
Thomas Burman	*,, 18*	*23*	*Unmarried*	*—*
John Mill	*,, 18*	*26*	*,,*	*27*
Henry Madge	*,, 19*	*32*		
Wm. Braund	*,, 21*	*70*	*Widower*	*27 Total*

and 3 strangers, Wm. Cloke, Jo. McCallum, and Ez. Johns. All were buried in the church-yard. A collection was organised in Bideford, Barnstaple, Torrington and Exeter. Total received = £2,994.2.6d.

During another bad storm in 1838, 21 men were drowned and 14 boats wrecked.

From the year 1840 herring fishing began to decline, trawling was just beginning. In 1841, we read of winter fish being herring, conger, whiting, hake, pollack and cod; in summer, turbot, sole, plaice, gurnet and mackerel.

Sadly names unknown of these Clovelly fishermen.

Our oldest fisherman, Oscar Abbott, died in 1976 aged 88. He only left the village to serve on a number of ships between the fishing seasons. He was active in fishing from his schooldays. At 13, he was still at school and would leave in the afternoon, run down to the harbour, jump into his father's boat and fish with him all night. Next morning, school called again, and he would talk of his eyes closing through tiredness. His wife laughingly told of his courting days, when he would fall asleep as they stood talking on the pier! Hard days indeed.

A little fishing still takes place. Fresh fish and shellfish are sold to the local hotels and restaurants and some sent over to France.

Nearly all the village boys were trained to be fishermen, as their fathers and forefathers were. When the winter fishing season was over, boats were pulled up away from the pounding waves. A rope would be attached to the boat and hauled away by many boys and men, who sang a sea-shanty between pulls. Some boats were left near the limekiln, others were taken through the archway or gatehouse, and away up the turnpike road. The sailors left Clovelly for the months between seasons, serving in ships and sailing to many lands.

Rest after toil (1903): Left to right: *Sam Shackson, Tom Jenn, "Ganger"* Harris, *William Moss, William Bate, Jim Jenn, John Cru se, 'Old' Steve Headon, Robert Hodge, Ambrose Pennington, Jamin Smale, Richard Cruse, Richard Foley, Richard Headon.*

I found some fishing snippets in Cory's chronicle of 1934. (He was an old man of Hartland who printed all the local news regularly until the 1940's).

1841 – "40 sailormen were absent when the count was taken, 950 were present." So, this would make a total of 990!

"21st Oct. 1858. From the "Journal". Clovelly boats caught 2½ maise/meas of herrings and sold in quantities of 9-11 for 6d."

"28th Nov. 1858. "The smack 'Margaret' of Falmouth went ashore at Harty Point in a heavy gale and became a total wreck. 2 bodies – supposed to be from the 'Margaret' – were picked up and buried at Abbotsham. A schooner put into Clovelly Bay in a disabled state."

1933. "150 years ago – 1883. Clovelly harbour light sanctioned with Trinity House by Neville Fane, Esq, JP bearing the whole cost and maintenance. From sunset to sunrise it shows a white light, except for 2 hours before and 2 hours after high-water. It was supplied by Chance & Co., Lighthouse Engineers, Nr. Birmingham."

1932. "Herring fishing is now in full swing. Nov. 7th – 1 boat had 5 or 6 meas. Badcock Bros. – crew of 3, ply to and fro from Bideford Quay in the 'Maggie' BD 14. They took a heavy catch on Friday morning and sold at 1d each.

12 boats with 2 men in each fish from Clovelly in 'picarooners.' This word is from the Mediterranean area and means pirates!"

Mr George Lamey quotes: "Mackerel were sold to Bideford for ¾d and retailed at 8d. Herrings went for 2/- a long hundred – 120."

Cory Burrows, responsible for the "Hartland Chronicle" – a copy of which he is handing to Jack Foley.

Charles Kingsley's famous poem was written as a result of the great fishing tragedy in Bideford Bay.

'Three fishers went sailing out into the West,
Out into the West as the sun went down.
Each thought of the woman who loved him the best
And children stood watching them out of the town.
For men must work and women must weep
And there's little to earn and many to keep
Tho' the harbour bar be moaning.

Three wives sat up in the lighthouse tower
And they trimmed the lamps as the sun went down.
They looked at the squall and they looked at the shower
And the night rack came rolling up – ragged and brown.
But men must work and women must weep
Tho' storms be sudden and waters deep
And the harbour bar be moaning.

Three corpses lay out on the shining sands
In the morning gleam as the moon went down,
And the women are mourning and wringing their hands
For those who will never come home to the town.
For men must work and women must weep
And the sooner it's over the sooner to sleep,
And goodbye to the bar and it's moaning."

His father when Rector, would go down and give comfort to the sorrowing relatives and often held a short service on the beach before the fishing fleet left. "Eternal Father" and Psalm 121 were great favourites.

"The Kingsley family were staying at Ilfracombe when Mr Hamlyn, of Clovelly Court, called and asked him to be his curate in 1831. 'Father' Charles gladly accepted." (They moved into 104 High Street, – a former beer house.) "Here lived father, mother, and six children for one year. The Rector died, and Mr Hamlyn appointed Mr Kingsley in his place. This meant moving up to the Rectory under the lovely old trees, with it's colony of rooks. Young Charles was now 11, and spent happy hours sitting up in an oak tree, which grew on a bank above the house. He would gaze out over the bay, an unbroken view in those days, and no doubt stories were already forming in his mind."

"As a family, they spent much time gathering shells and searching out wild flowers. They loved to ride, too. Eventually, Chelsea called them and sadly, they left Clovelly. Charles returned many times and usually stayed at 'Jessamine Cottage'."

(Charles Kingsley, His Life and Letters, by his wife.)

"The Luff"—A famous painting by J. Hook, RA, done in 1856 and hung in the Royal Academy 1858, showing John Cruse, Richard Pengelly, and Bill Burman.

"Elinor Roget" the last rowing boat

1937 – Lifeboat crew and launchers – with the "City of Nottingham".

Lifeboats

Various lifeboats, nine in all, have done wonderful service in the bay. There was no lifeboat here until 1870. Before that the noble coastguards did wonderful service, but their vessel was a "gig" – a long light boat with oars or sail, and quite unworthy of rounding the headland and "the race of Harty".

The first lifeboat was 33 feet long, rowed by ten oars, held fifteen crewmen, and was named *"Alex and Matilda Boetefeur"*. A boathouse was constructed but when a larger vessel replaced the rowing type, the shed had to be enlarged accordingly. The first boat soon proved herself by rescuing a fishing crew; so many had previously lost their lives in fishing disasters.

A list of boats, coxswains and crews, along with exciting photographs, total of launches and lives saved, can be seen in the old boathouse during the summer months. The Ladies Lifeboat Guild (formed in 1936) also run a stall in the lifeboat house, raising cash for the Institution.

A change came about in 1968. The old type of boat was taken away to work in an easier area, and we were given a fine vessel, 70 foot all-steel cruising type, "70-001 *Charles H. Barrett*". She cost £57,000 and has a range of 750 miles. How different from the first boat at £320! Since 1968, other improved boats have been tried out in Clovelly Bay, and now we see a newer model, given by the City of Bristol, and called by this name. A crew of five man her at all times. A helicopter often supports the boat on a rescue mission, and so together, they continue to "rescue life at sea".

Charles Kingsley's "Three Fishers" poem, and the harbour light, remind us of two fishing tragedies in the bay, in 1821 and 1838. Many ships have ended their days in the bay. Several lie quite near the shore and their skeletons could be seen a few years back if the water was clear.

In 1906 a Spanish ship, the *"Arbril"* , went ashore in the fog. The crew took to their boat and rowed up to the Red Lion Hotel. There, the landlord, Mr J.T Moss provided food and shelter for the night and their travelling money to London. The Shipwrecked Mariners Fund paid all these expenses. (There is still a collecting box in use, outside a cottage next to the New Inn). Two years later, the *"Huddersfield"* suffered the same fate. She was a collier, and had left South Wales with only one member of the crew sober! Her chances were pretty slender in thick fog. The crew took to their boats, one of which rowed to the Red Lion. The Clovelly lifeboat was launched, and she rescued the other boat.

A severe storm and tidal wave occurred about 1912. Much damage was done to the Red Lion, skylights were smashed, and water poured down the staircase. An old lady living in a cottage at the rear was rescued, and carried through the archway to safety.

1962 – Launching the Lifeboat to go to the assistance of the "Green Ranger".

Easter lilies.

The Parish Church of "All Saints"

The most important building in Clovelly! A sweeping statement, maybe, but here prayer has been offered for 1,000 years, and it is indeed hallowed ground. We must leave our car at the church gates, (bottom of Slerra Hill), and walk a few yards down to the lych-gate, (lych = coffin = a place to rest it before it is carried into church.) There is a date scratched on the left-hand wall here, 1636, probably the work of Will Cary. We take the right-hand path and walk under a lovely avenue of yews, five on each side, with snowdrops beneath in early Spring. The yews were planted by Mrs Hamlyn's parents in 1863. Over the porch is a seventeenth century sundial. The arch here is Norman, and once was at the entrance to the earlier church, which was tiny and rather plain.

Go through the main door and down a couple of steps, – stop and look toward the centre or nave. Beneath three huge granite pillars is a block of pews. Under here, in 1957/58 when a new floor was being laid, we found a wall, 4 feet thick. Dr. Spinks' (then Rector) theory was confirmed by experts that it was most likely part of the Norman church; red sand-stone, four feet wide, and stretching from the back of the pews to the other end of this central block. He estimated that it would run south and then west back toward the south door again. I found this very exciting, as I had just succeeded my mother on the Parochial Church Council, but so frustrating as we could see no more! Two stone 'coffin-tombs' were unearthed, one complete with skeleton, – the other held only a skull. Priests were buried inside a church, so if the building stood as Dr. Spinks suggested one priest was buried inside, and the other outside, beyond a pillar. I feel that the original church lay in the opposite areas, (i.e. north aisle and Lady Chapel). When my cousin, Alan Johns, was laying a new floor here in 1974, he uncovered two feet of a Norman-shaped doorway. Again, we know no more. Pehaps sufficient money will be provided to excavate properly one day.

Our font dates from about 1000–1050, so we have plenty of evidence of an earlier church. Another font-bowl, not as old, rests on the floor beneath the list of patrons and rectors. It was serving as a pig trough when recognised. We are not sure which chapel it served, as there were several both in this parish and neighbouring Hartland.

We stand in awe and wonder in the church. How did the five huge granite pillars come over from Lundy, 600 years ago? Shaping them could not have been an easy task, either.

The delightful roof carved from large chunks of timber, is certainly built to last. I well remember climbing a rather shaky ladder at seven o'clock one morning, to take a picture of the damage from "death-watch beetle". I lay flat on the scaffolding and was shocked to see so much destruction to the beams. After treatment in 1973, we should be safe for another twenty years, the previous spraying being in 1953. After the Rentokil team had finished, the ceiling between the beams was whitened in memory of a parishioner.

The north aisle is the oldest, about 1370. The south aisle and chancel probably came into being a few years later, – the building enlarging according to finance and growing congregations.

The solid oak pews glow with love and care, but until 1961 the woodwork looked dry and almost grey. Willing helpers and pints of linseed oil soon restored them. In the course of two weeks, a team of men and women cleaned and redecorated the entire church, at no cost to the parishioners.

The **pew-ledges** now hold hymn and prayer books, but were once used as fire-arm rests. Men carried them always, as many would have to walk miles on lonely roads.

Candle brackets slot into holes cut in some pew-ledges; this was once the only form of lighting, and now used to light the church for the Midnight Mass at Christmas.

We have four **doorways**, the north and south being the oldest. The heavy studded door leading into the north aisle, had gun-shot removed from it a while ago, but we have no record of how/why the shots were embedded. There is much space between the door and it's arch, and a northerly wind blows in from time to time! Otherwise, our oil-fired heating system is effective. The south door is quite impressive and creaks when opened, almost asking to be treated with respect owing to its great age. The west or tower door was the idea of Mrs Hamlyn. It was placed there in the late 1880's, and she entered through it on her wedding day in 1889.

Services. We have much more comfort than our ancestors, however. The first worshippers only had a huge space to stand and pray. The preacher would move about the church, seeking the warmest spot, – the congregation would close in on him and keep warm, too!

In 1603, it became law for a **pulpit** to be installed. 1634 saw Will Cary setting an example. His oak pulpit was fixed on a deal base, to the right (south) side of the church.

In 1644, **organs** were banned from churches, and orchestras sufficed. In 1889, an organ was purchased and placed on the site of the pulpit, the latter having been moved to it's present position, and fixed on a granite plinth. The then owner of Lundy, Mrs Heaven, presented this, and a local boatman, Mr Moss, shipped it across.

Monuments and Memorials. We have thirteen windows of varying dates and patterns. All the stained glass is in memory of people connected with the church or Clovelly.

Three brass monuments are set in the floor a few yards from the High Altar. Robert Cary is represented as a knight in armour; the second is another figure in armour, but larger; the third is a bishop's crosier.

On the window-ledge set in the north-east chancel wall, we see a small black plaque engraved with a skeleton and spade. This is in memory of Anne Cary, who died when only eight months old.

Many stone tablets are secured to the church walls, dedicated to Carys and Hamlyns, and one to Wm. Cooke. General and Mrs Asquith are remembered, their plaque being found on the west wall. His medals are encased below. Christine Hamlyn's lovely memorial is next to this. My own parents' names, Paul and Gladys, are engraved on a small tablet over 'their' seat, near the south door.

The space to the right of the High Altar is filled with a high tomb monument, in memory of Robert Cary 1586.

Many slate memorials are set in the red-tiled flooring of the aisles. The lettering is almost unreadable in most cases.

Vaults. The sexton of 1863/6 recorded the fact that beneath the altar steps lie twelve coffins, in three rows of four. They are probably Cary bodies. Some of the family would have been buried at Cockington, their other estate.

The Hamlyn vault is under the Lady Chapel. Christine Hamlyn's parents were placed inside in 1869, to rest beside four other coffins, then it was walled up.

The Bells.

The Font. This has been damaged at some time, a slice being hacked off. The back is flat as though it had once leaned against a wall. We know that prior to its present position, under the tower arch, it stood in front of a pillar which is halfway between the north and south doors. Here, many a baby has received it's baptismal blessings.

Our **records** only go back as far as 1686, baptisms, marriages and burials alike. We think the Court fire of 1680 must have destroyed the earlier records. Now, all precious records are kept in the County archives.

The **tower** is now incorporated, but once stood alone. We understand the base to be of Norman work, and that the upper section was rebuilt in the 13th century. We have six bells which are rung each Sunday. They make a mellow sound, and we think are the best in the Deanery.

The weight of the tenor bell is 10 cwt. – dated 1900.
The weight of the fifth bell is 7 cwt. – dated 1758.
The weight of the fourth bell is 5¾ cwt. – dated 1758.
The weight of the third bell is 5 cwt. – dated 1758.
The weight of the second bell is 4 cwt. – dated 1895.
The weight of the first bell is 3 cwt. – dated 1905.

The original date cannot be told. We know that four were re-cast in 1758 and one more added. The sixth (tenor) arrived in 1900 to complete the set. 1933 saw them re-cast and re-hung at great expense to the parish. Our ringers have gained many certificates, which cover the tower walls.

The bells not only call us to worship, but celebrate a wedding or toll for a funeral. Long ago, the Lord of the manor had his workers summoned by the ringing of a bell. The bell was also a warning of fire, or enemy attack in time of war.

Like other towers in the Westcountry, water has seeped through many times. Hardly a decade has passed without complaints and attempted repair work at enormous cost.

Rooks nest in two colonies, one near the church, the other by the Rectory. The sound of these birds is one which some love and feel that nothing has changed in Clovelly whilst others carry a gun and endeavour, (quite unlawfully), to shoot them.

Cobbled pathway to Clovelly Church.

A well-kept **churchyard** surrounds the building. Since most of the old curb-stones have been removed, the caretaker's work is a little easier, and the overall effect a great improvement. We hope to stand some older head-stones against the surrounding walls. Every year people return to search for their ancestors' names. This yard was closed in 1948, when a new burial ground was opened a few yards up the path. In 1736, cobbles formed the path around the churchyard. It looks charming in an old photo, but no date or reason is given for the change we now see.

Small, bracket-seats, known as pauper-pews, are fixed to the end of three pews near the tower arch. There were three more on the block facing us, but they were in a poor condition and removed. Pauper children sat on these tiny uncomfortable seats. It would seem as though many suffered in this parish, – we read of 'a poor school' and 'poor-pots' during the 1800's.

Ugly box-pews, and one or two huge galleries filled the back (west end) of the church, until the great restoration of 1863 to 1866. The Rev W Prince was rector 1687-1715, and seating is quoted 'for 350'. (Congregations had increased by now.) One gallery would have housed the orchestra. I quote from the churchwardens account book:- "In 1796, William Nickell was training the musicians and singers. He received three pound three shilling the first year and one guiney for the years after"

Lighting. Our lovely wrought iron lamps cost £3 each in 1895/6, and were paid for by public subscriptions. They were fed by oil, but now from an electricity supply. They give a subdued lighting effect and the church looks beautiful. Early in the morning is a good time to be inside, too, when sunlight streams through the east window.

Lovely hand-worked **frontals** adorn the altars. Mrs Hamlyn's sisters are commemorated by the purple and white ones. Eveline Hamlyn-Fane was working on the white one, and had embroidered the lower half when her final illness prevented the completion. Wippells of Exeter actualy carried out the remaining work. It was blessed and used in 1910. This is used for the special seasons of Christmas, Easter, and All Saints Day. In 1957, the Wantage Sisters entirely re-mounted this lovely work of soft colours, old rose, gold, blue and shades of green.

The purple one consists of embroidery taken off the original white frontal. Mrs A M Jones, a retired school teacher, restored it again in the early 1960's. This we use in Advent and Lent.

The green frontal is used for all the other weeks of the year. The design is unusual, grapes embroidered in silver and gold, and peacocks with 'jewelled ' eyes. Again, the colours are most appealing. A priceless piece of embroidery was purchased in Italy by Mrs Hamlyn and made into an altar frontal in 1900. It is of green material, covered in embroidery of the softest colourings, and considered to be work of Verona, at least 300 years old. Unfortunately, Mrs Jones found that no more repairs could be done to it. She darned it, and finally stitched a covering of green net all over it. It has lasted extremely well.

Our "Dorcas" also created a purple frontal for use in Lent and Advent, and one of cream brocade with a rose emblem embroidered in shades of pink, and studded with 'jewels', for use at Christmas and Easter. These complete a liturgical set for the Lady Chapel.

Needless to say, two fine frontals in St Peter's Chapel are also of her craftsmanship – purple, bearing the crossed keys of St Peter, and a white one, of very old embroidery stitched on new material. Annie May Jones died in 1986.

A green cover was made by Mrs Abbott many years ago, and now has gold keys added, also the work of Mrs Jones. All over the Parish Church we see her creations, lace, tatting, hassocks and kneelers, and in the vestry, Communion sets, and a cope of gold and white. (St Peter's has 19 red and gold and each hassock represents a former worshipper). A Guild of Workers have recently made woollen hassocks to replace our rexine ones, – wool being warmer to the knees. The original altar-table was too low for the Rev Wm Harrison. He had it moved into the vestry, and the present larger version replaced it in 1884. When St Peter's Chapel was opened in 1948, the little altar seemed appropriate. It was taken down to the chapel until a new table was made in 1958. Finally, the original table returned to the Parish Church, and settled down in the new Lady Chapel.

Many brass articles have been given over the years. The eagle lectern, (which is so time-consuming to clean!) Altar vases given by Mrs Harrison, altar cross, book-rest, and candlesticks, all in memory of someone. The brass ewer which stands on the font platform, was the result of many people giving sixpence each in 1903.

A cane-seated **chair** is thought to be of the time of Charles II; it can be seen inside the altar rails. Opposite is a plush-seated chair, and both are used when we have visiting clergy or bishops.

Near here, on the narrow door set in the north-east wall, is fixed an **iron cross.** It was given to Christine Hamlyn and is said to have originated in Constantinople. The suggestion that it dates from the third century is rather exaggerated, we feel. The **hour glass** standing near the pulpit was given to the church by Will Cary in 1635, a year after he had built the pulpit. The hour glass disappeared and was considered lost for ever, but, in 1921, a Dr Ryder Richardson returned it. It now stands in an iron cage given by Mrs Hamlyn, and Mr Lott, estate foreman, carved the stand from wood washed up on the beach. We now time the service each Sunday, but originally, the sermon alone lasted one hour!

The red **carpet** was a gift from Mr Hamlyn. It came from India in 1901.

Other decorations and pieces of furniture have been donated in memory of a friend or relative. Our list is endless! This is indeed 'the House of God' and we are grateful.

A vellum hangs near the tower arch showing the names of priests who have served the present church.

1262 – R. Gifford
1280 – W. de Peifnton
1308 – R. de Dolburghe
1338 – D. Angeline
1339 – O. de Staunton
1362 – W. Payne
(W. Crabbe – Curate)
1397 – R. Loman
1407 – W. Penwonan
1411 – R. Plenya
(Edmund Kene – Curate)
1462 – W. Danzall
(J. Husband – Curate)
1503 – J. Clymowe
1505 – H. Plymton
1531 – T. Herle
1554 – T. Brown
1559 – T. Herle
1589 – W. Tooker
1601 – R. Thome
1632 – W. Yeo
1639 – G. Cary
1668 – O. Naylor
1687 – W. Prince
1715 – O. Jones
1730 – J. Robbins
1777 – C. Hammett
1782 – R. Hammett
1796 – L. Lewis
1826 – O.W.H. Williams
(C. Kingsley – Curate)
1832 – C. Kingsley
1836 – Z.H. Drake
1856 – J.J. Chichester
1883 – Wm. Harrison
1897 – F.G. Phillips
1899 – T.L.V. Simkins
1932 – P. Somers-Cock
1938 – R.P. Cavendish
1945 – A.S. Chandler
1952 – P. Geake
1955 – G.S. Spinks
1959 – R.O.H. Eppingstone
1980 – D. Bates

Sadly 1980 brought to an end the Ellis record of 80 years service to the Church in Clovelly as Church Wardens and Church Council members.

The following extract is taken from a list of patrons who were Lords of the Manor, who presented a priest to the living of Clovelly, hence the fact that we have more than one date for some owners.

Richard Gifford	1286
Edith, Lady of Clovelly	1308
John de Staunton	1338
Robert Mandeville	1339
John Mandeville	1362
Wm Cary	1397
Thomasine	1411
Sir Wm Cary	1462
Robt Cary	1503
John Gilbert	1505
Robt Cary, Esq	1531
Queen Elizabeth 1st	1589
Margaret Cary (widow)	1601
Will Cary, Esq	1632
Dr George Cary	1668
Will Cary Esq	1687
Robt Cary	1715
Robt Barber mar Eliz Cary	1730
James Hamlyn, Esq.	1777
,, ,, ,,	1782
Sir James, 1st Baronet	1796
,, 2nd ,,	1826
,, 3rd ,,	1832
,, 3rd ,,	1836
,, 3rd ,,	1856
Neville Hamlyn Fane	1883
Mrs. Christine Hamlyn	1897
,,	1899
,,	1932
Hon. Mrs. B C Asquith	1938
,,	1945
,,	1952
,,	1955
,,	1959

The list of Rectors begins at 1262 and quotes – "Incumbents for former church – not known". A document in the Vatican Library dated 1393 states:

"Boniface IX in the year 1393 to the Archbishop of Canterbury confirming the foundation by William Cary of the Collegiate Church for seven priests and for twenty-four nuns of the Order of St. Clare of Clovelly".
(Oliver's Monastican – Exeter Cathedral Library).

Sadly, we have no further record, and think that either William died before the Collegiate Church was formed and his family did not carry out his wishes, or that the scheme was proving to be too costly. In any case, it would have been destroyed at the time of the dissolution of the monasteries and the revenue seized by the Crown. The Assistant Librarian from the Vatican visited Clovelly at the beginning of **this** century, and confirmed that the actual building did not take place.

We find the following in the Bishops' Transcripts, (time of Bishop Edmund Stafford):-

"Clovelly. Chapel of St. Giles.
Abbot in the parish of. licensed for 3yrs – 15 Feb 1401-2
William Penwonam R – 6 Sept 1407
Richard Plenya R – 1 June 1417
Walter Jodel Chaplain Licensed to preach in the Parish Church
19 Feb 1411-12"

Again we have unanswered questions.

Clovelly Rectory. In the archives is an old terrier concerning this. A great survey was carried out in the diocese of Exeter, – completed by 1680.

"Clovelly Rectory – A true and perfect Terrier 20 April 1680.

A hall. A parlour adjoins. A chamber over the the parlour.
A porch. A closet over the porch.
A pantry. A chamber over the pantry. A little closet adjoins.
A kitchen. A chamber over the kitchen.
A cole house. A chamber over the cole house.
A malting house. A chamber over the malting house.
A dairy. A chamber over the dairy.
A brew house. A malting room over and a malt kiln adjoining.
3 pigge houses.
A fair large stoning barne.
A stable and a chamber over it for servants.
Another stable for the worke horses.
A shippen and a tallet over it.

Glebeland.

An orchard – *about ½ acre.*
Berry Meadow *about 4 acres.*
Yellery – *about 1 acre.*
Southern Yellery – *about 9 acres.*
Northern Yellery – *about 9 acres.*
A little meadow adjoining Nthn. Yellery – about ½ an acre.
Shutt Close – *fower acres.*
The Barne Park – *6 acres.*
Easter Cole – *4 acres.*
Wester Cole – *4 acres.*
A wood upon the clift – *about 6 acres.*
More called Buddlemore – *30 acres.*
A little more on the sth. side of the highway leading to Stitworthy called Buddlemore – 2 acres.

Signed: Oliver Naylor – Rector
B. Cooke) Ch. Wdns.
J. Cooke)

A thatched roof covered at least one part of this building. The present rectory was built in 1790 from rubble and stones left over from the Court fire of 1789. The 1680 dwelling could have been where the Old Rectory Cottage stands this being part of the old structure. In 1909 when work was being carried out on this cottage, the walls proved to be several feet thick, and not in proportion to an ordinary cottage. "Quaint panelled cupboards in the walls must date back much further than 1790," quotes T.L.V. Simkin in 1910/1909.

An aerial view of Clovelly Dykes.

Clovelly Dykes

"In North Devon is a small group of hill-forts of which "Clovelly Dykes", on the plateau above Barnstaple Bay, looking across to the coast of South Wales, is the most striking. An immense series of ramparts covering a greater area than any other hill-fort in Devon except 'Milber'. Milber stands on the brow rather than the summit of the hill, it's triple defences with wide spaces between them compensate for this military weakness. Clovelly Dykes is a similar but more elaborate type of settlement of the same period which has not yet been excavated. The 1st century BC is probably the date Iron Age B. It is these people who mainly constitute the 'Dumnonii' the people of the land".
(Survey of Devon. Prof. W.G. Hoskins).

We know little about the Dykes, which are about 700 feet above the sea, and approximately 20 acres in size. The living quarters were most likely in the centre huts of wattle and daub covered with thatched rooves. Deep ditches were dug out and the earth piled up to form ramparts. We think three circular defence banks surrounded the central area. It is difficult to plan the shape as so much ploughing has taken place over the years; a farm was actually built on part of it, and worse still, the road into Clovelly, leaving a section of the Dykes isolated. A "mazy" plan gave the feeling of security, and a stone or wooden stockade could have fenced in the entire camp.

"We know that no road approached from the south. (Bude direction), possibly because of bogs draining not having taken place. It's purpose could have been purely defensive or for worship, perhaps of the "Sun-god" or some other primitive deity. It has been suggested that as many as three hundred people might have taken ten years to construct it allowing for bad weather and tribal wars".
(Clovelly Dykes, Carter 1927).

So a community was dwelling in "Ditchen-hills" in what is known as the Iron Age. Where they came from and where they went, we cannot tell.

A local, man, Mr Godwin, once studied the formation of the Dykes, and found a few scraps of evidence, cooking pits, some charcoal, and pot-sherds in the inner circle, also a few flint-flakes. He presented the remnants to the Bideford Museum. The mystery remains; even if the people were from Northern France and lived in 100 BC how do we account for the flints, which date from a much earlier period? The last word comes from the Rev S. Baring-Gould, who writes after an almost fruitless dig at Clovelly Dykes in July 1903:

"As far as can be judged, it was raised in The Iron Age, which began about 800 BC. Iron cannon balls of the time of the Commonwealth have also been found (1648). A great number of rounded pebbles for sling-stones were discovered. Flint flakes (from Dorset?) for flint arrowheads, probably, could date from the Bronze Age. Some modern pottery and fire-holes full of charcoal were found. Ploughing has harmed the site. The moats have been much deeper, the bottom of one moat was not found although a six-foot trench was dug."

Definition of Clovelly and Farm Names

Let us take a look at the name "Clovelly". The Oxford Dictionary of Place-names quotes:-

Clovelie – 1080 Domesday Book
Clovely – 1242 Book of Fees
Cloveli – 1276 Inquisi iones post mortem
Colfely – 1290 Charter Rolls

Clovelly is only two miles from Velly, spelt

Felye – 1287
Over-Felye – 1301
La-Feley – 1333

Clovelly is no doubt Velly with the Old English Cloh or Clof meaning 'ravine'. Velly or Felye, was apparently the name of the semi-circular ridge on or by which the places are so called on account of a fancied likeness to the felly (Old English 'felg') of a wheel. (Clo' in Clovelly, refers to the ravine at whose bottom end the village is. Actually Velly is in Hartland parish, being situated on the farther side of a stream forming part of the parish boundary.

I have found four other ways of spelling the name Clovelly:-

Clouvely – 1361
Clavellegh – 1535
Clavelly – 1630
Clavelleigh – 1800

and there could be more on old maps.

The Saxon conquest in the south took place about the year 454 AD and the race of Dumnonii is mentioned in the first century AD.

"A British monk named Gildas in 547 wrote a plea for help against un-named barbarians. He was a great historian and names a kingdom of Dumnonii – whose memory survives in the name of 'Devon'. This kingdom was still in existence in 710 when Geraint was reported King". It is clear that the Saxon conquest of Devon was followed by an extensive influx of population westwards, from regions already settled".
(Oxford History of England. Sir F. Stenton).

"The Saxon hordes poured over the hills and vales, cut their way through thick forests, felled the trees and built homesteads where they tilled the land and reared their cattle. They came in clans or families, and settled wherever their ships took them".
(English Villages. P.H. Ditchfield).

At least we know that the Saxons were our first farmers. They formed the hundreds or parish boundaries; manors existed in their time, and we could imagine Clovelly as such before the Normans came, although manor **is** *a Norman word.*

"The Manor of 'Clovelie' is reported to have been part of the Saxon earldom of Gloucester and belonged to one called 'Britric'. Poor Britric was very unfortunate. When an ambassador to Baldwin of Flanders, he refused to marry Baldwin's daughter – Matilda. The slighted lady became the consort of William the Conqueror. In revenge for her despised love, she caused poor Britric to be imprisoned in Winchester – where he eventually died. His lands were all confiscated and some given to the Queen".
(Devonshire Notes & Queries 1830-40).

In 1083 when the Domesday Survey began, Clovelly was being farmed for the King by "Goscelm". It is obvious that besides the manor house, farms existed, probably near the house. No description is available of any buildings, nor yet if a church or chapel had been built.

A number of hamlets and some thousands of single farmsteads came into existence between 1150 and 1350 according to Prof. Hoskins.

In Higher Clovelly and within a radius of two miles, we have thirteen 'dwellings' which date from this period. Our twentieth century titles are not very much different:-

Kynwarlande	1201	–	Kennerland 1900's
Stotteworth	1238	–	Stitworthy ,,
Estcote	1281	–	Eastacott ,,
Snackeslonde	1301	–	Snackland ,,
La Slade	1316	–	Slade ,,
Bornestone	1319	–	Burnstone ,,
Thornwurthi	1330	–	Thornery ,,
Hewurthi	1330	–	Highworthy ,,
Burforde	1330	–	Burford ,,
Hokylputt	1330	–	Hugglepit ,,
Dounelonde	1330	–	Downland ,,
Wykenebiry	1330	–	Wrinkleberry ,,
West Dick	1333	–	Dyke ,,

Fruit Stall on the Square – my aunt and "helper".

The Lameys lived in part of the house built across the street, "Temple Bar" or "The Bow", reputed to be one of the oldest in Clovelly. The outer walls remain, but the interior has been gutted. Tiny staircases led up to the roof and there certainly was an odd feeling in the attic, not improved by dim lighting!

The only other cottage in which I felt this uncanny sensation was at No 105. The old tenant told me that she had seen ghosts, (two old seamen), in the top room. Old beams, one part of a boat, thick cob walls, and almost dark, – yes, those old men could have haunted there. She did not know, however, that previous residents had been seafaring folk, by the name of Jewell. Most of the old Jewell family had dark hair, were fairly tall, and their noses were very Spanish in shape. The legend of Bucks' Spaniards would have fitted the Jewells even better. So many years of breeding have passed since the Armada, it is almost impossible to find any resemblance now, – if the story were true.

Lily Braund, now Edwards, whose father rowed here from Bucks, has told me some fascinating tales of her childhood. I quote her own words:

"Two men used to bring a gramophone and play it in the street, just below Rats' Castle, (near the limekiln). They collected money in a hat. One tune they always played was, 'Ain't it grand, to be blooming well dead.'" "Mr Cudmore had a stall near the New Inn. He sold fruit and vegetables. Lots of people used to sell in the street until they brought in a law in 1932 to stop them. We could buy proper cream for 6d a quarter, butter for 1/- a lb, and eggs was ever so cheap. A gipsy went from door to door with a basket of old-fashioned clothes pegs for sale. Florrie Burrows brought oil from Hartland, and "Daddy Monday" – do you remember his long beard? He sold boot-laces, tape, cotton and all sorts."

"The donkeys used to stand in sixes on the beach, just below the limekiln. As two donkeys moved away carrying people, (who had to be below 9 stone), two more were brought around from behind the Red Lion, – 'twas more shady there. Once a year, an inspection was held. All the animals were groomed and their shoes polished. Braids would be threaded through their manes, and the best ones received a prize." "Father helped to unload people from the steamers, the biggest number was 1,200 in one day and there was five steamers. Nearly every house did bed and breakfast, twas 3/- and 3/6 in they days. Heaps of em did teas and luncheons, there was lobster, crab, prawns and ham. Raspberries, strawberries and cream (what a mixture). All the houses was properly white-washed with lime, the father's did and they borrowed each others ladders. Outside one place was a flag-pole and the flag said 'Bed & Breakfast Teas Seaview' and 3 or 4 maids served the teas inside and out in the small garden. Father used to sell prawns at 1/6 for a hundred, you could buy a ¼ hundred ½ hundred or 1 x hundred."

Mrs. Cudmore selling produce.

Legends and Stories

Much legend has been woven around us – piracy, smuggling, wrecking, Spaniards – the Braunds of Bucks being direct descendents of Spanish survivors. Only a few customs survive and I'll tell you also of some which have perished.

Shrove Tuesday is "Lanshard" or "Lent-sherd Night". As soon as dusk comes, the children meet at the top of the street. Each one will have brought a metal article tied with a long string, maybe a couple of old tins, a bucket, oil-drum, anything up to an old bath-tub. These they drag along, up and down the street, running faster and faster, sparks flying, uttering whoops of joy, until it is time for the smaller children to go to bed. This shocking noise is supposed to drive the devil out of the village before Lent begins and everyone settles down to be good for forty days!

Palm Sunday. We have a donkey, sometimes a foal and a group of donkeys in church. The Rector places his cope over the back of one donkey, and gives each child a branch of bamboo, to represent palm. We process out of the tower door and move around the churchyard, then walk to the Court. Here, a lesson is read and prayers said. Another hymn brings us back inside again, just like the first Palm Sunday.

Palm Sunday procession.

April Fool Day – 1st April. Someone creeps around the village pinning humorous notices on the doors of people known to see the funny side.

May Morning – 1st May, would be observed by girls who rose at dawn, walked through the Hobby or over the parklands and washed their faces in dew.

Blessings – The first Sunday in January is Plough Sunday. Farmers come to church and ask God's blessing on their work on the land. We have an old plough near the lych-gate as a permanent reminder.

Rogation Sunday. The Sunday before the Ascension, we move around the parish offering prayers, readings and hymns on different ground each year.

Harvest Thanksgiving. This is the last "crop" service and is usually held at the beginning of October.

1st November – All Saints Day. My mother began a custom to celebrate this date, the Patronal Festival of the Parish Church. A service was followed by showing 8mm films of the years activities, both connected with church life and within the parish. She then began taking 35mm slides and I continued in her footsteps by photographing everything we did or organised. Almost everyone had taken part and turned up to see themselves. Great fun – but eventually too costly to continue.

The Sea. This is blessed from small boats bobbing about in the harbour, carrying the congregation. A Sunday is chosen in summer, to suit the in-tide. Prayers are offered for all fishermen, lifeboat crews and "all who go down to the sea in ships".

Father Christmas appears at various parties and walks up and down the village on Christmas Eve, leaving presents for the children.

"Lansherd" – local children noisily driving the Devil away!

New Year's Eve Service – Methodist Chapel. This was observed faithfully until a few years ago. Previous to this, for many years, a portable organ was carried around after the service, set up at various points in the village and the people sang "Count your many blessings, name them one by one".

Brides always walk up the cobbled street, their bridesmaids walking behind. After the ceremony in church, the newly-married couple walk down and the guests process behind – a pretty sight. Sometimes the donkeys accompany them – bedecked in silken flowers and coloured ribbon.

At Christmas-tide, carol singers usually travel around the parish, singing from door to door. Hartland Town Band arrives and try to find a stand under a street light. It sometimes rains, and this makes us more grateful for their noble efforts. A lovely custom only lasted a few years – Christmas trees outside cottages, at strategic points in the High Street, lit with outdoor lights. One shower of rain or a strong wind would quickly fuse a bulb, and leave the tree in darkness. Eventually it became too costly to continue.

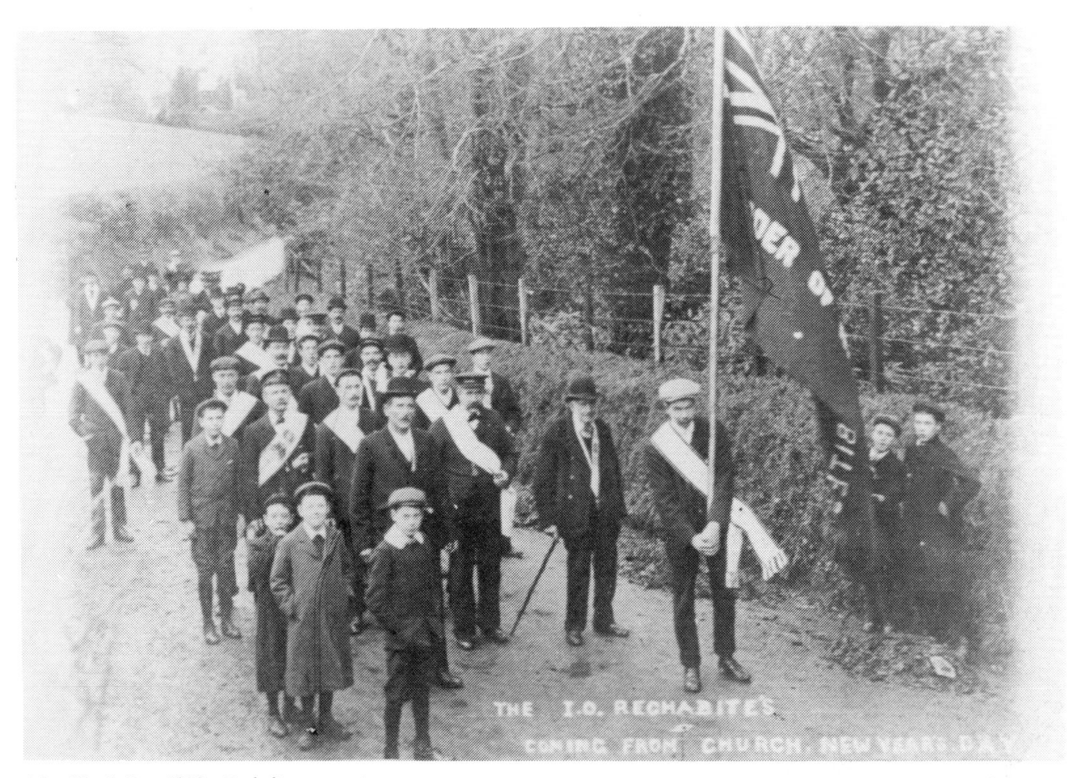

New Year's Day 1909 – Rechabites procession.

Jack Whitefield marries Lily Meadow.

Interesting Events and Dates

There is a blood-curdling story concerning a family who are supposed to have dwelt in Clovelly about 250 years ago.

"John Gregg and his family of Robbers and Murderers, who took up their abode in a cave near to the seaside in Clovelly in Devonshire, where they lived 25 years without so much as once going to visit any city or town. How they robbed above 1,000 persons and murdered and ate all whom they robbed. How at last they were happily discovered by a pack of bloodhounds, and how John Gregg, his wife, 8 sons, 6 daughters, 18 grandsons and 14 grand-daughters, (48 of them in all), were all seized and executed by being cast alive into three fires and were burnt.

As soon as they had robbed and murdered any man, woman or child, they used to carry off their carcases to their den, – where, cutting them into quarters they would pickle the mangled limbs and afterward, eat them, it being their subsistance.

The place they inhabited was solitary and when the tide came up, it reached a mile underground so that when some had come armed, they passed by the mouth of the cave without any notice.

A man and his wife behind him on the same horse coming one evening from a fair, and falling into an ambuscade of those wretches, they attacked him in a furious manner. The man to save himself – fought bravely, riding some of 'em down by main force, but in the conflict, the poor woman fell from behind him and was instantly murdered before his face. The female cannibals cutting her throat and sucking her blood with as great gusto as though it had been wine. This done, they ripped her up through and pulled out her entrails: which dismal spectacle caused the man to make the more resistance. It pleased Providence while he was engaged, thirty people came in a body together from a fair, on which John Gregg and his crew withdrew and made the best of the way through a wood to their den."

(The History of John Gregg and his Family of Robbers and Murderers – Bodleian Library, Oxford).

The rest of the story tells us that Exeter sent 400 men and a pack of hounds who tracked down the cannibals, took them to Exeter and next day to Plymouth, where they were burnt, first having their hands and feet cut off.

There is a strong theory that "Dingle Hole" in the Hobby was the entrance. Mr Oscar Abbott told of the time he and friends ventured a short way in and down this narrow "tomb-like entrance." It was very dark inside so they struck matches and lit a candle. Soon the air became unbearable and the candle went out. They dropped stones and heard them falling down a long way toward the beach. There were huge black spiders, and many bats flew around them. The entrance has long since fallen in, but I was lucky enough to see it.

The next date in history seems dull in comparison, but it is good to know a bit about our past.

In the period covered by the "Old Churchwarden's Account Book 1750-1809" (as recorded in 1900 Magazine,) church expenses were met by a rate, and the churchwardens being parish officers, many things were paid for from this fund which had nothing whatever to do with the church, but would nowadays come upon the Poor Rate or be dealt with by the parish and District Councils. Some of the items are decidedly interesting and throw light upon forgotten parish history and customs of the time.

The churchwardens were generally elected once a year. The churchyard was apparently cut once a year, and the fortunate man who did the work was paid 1/- for his task!

Four shillings was paid annually for cleaning the church and someone – probably the sexton – had 4/- a year for whipping the dogs, (we suppose keeping them out of church.)

Each year the churchwardens presented a bill for destroying foxes and badgers or "baggers". It would seem that the former were held the more destructive creatures, as the price paid for a dead badger was only 1/-, whilst a vixen cost the parish 5/- and a dog-fox 2/6d.

In 1759, some of the church bells were re-cast, the bill for which was £61 0s 6d.

Holy Communion was only celebrated four times in the year, at Easter, Whitsuntide, Michaelmas and Christmas, but the number of communicants was very large. (How I wish we had more records such as these.)

1800 There is a school for boys.
1808 Poor received dripping and food in a "Poor Pot."
(This pot was of china, had a lid and two handles. A leather strap was slotted through. It was filled from the Court kitchen and distributed to many.) This custom was clearly remembered by Mrs Abbott, when over 80.
1826 The pier was lengthened and a breakwater built to protect it.
1826/9 (From an Account Book found in old Church Magazine:-)
Rev Orlando Williams – Rector.
Church Choir – Mr Ashton played violen-cello.
Singers – 15 men and 1 boy.
8 women and 1 girl = 25.

A large choir, but all did not attend regularly. One farmer only comes to church once a quarter. Not all the voices are pleasant, – one was said to be very noisy!

Poor to come at 10 every Wednesday morning for pot liquor and dripping, etc.

The parish sense of justice was stirred by a tradesman thrashing his apprentice severely for refusing to steal wood!

1826 *A good many women at that time took part in manual labour, some working in the Hobby, which was being made.*
Betty Pickard's daughter, whose husband had deserted her, carried coals up on her back and has worked this year at the restoration of the pier. She received the same wages as her strength was equal.(T L V Simkins adds; 'Perhaps she had been roughly handled by her husband?')

1855 *Jo Burrow appointed Superintendent of the Clovelly highways. Jo Jewell and John Eddy – Poor Wardens.*

1858 *The Luff painting hung in the Academy. (The old man is Will Burman; the young man John Cruse, whose mother was Charles Kingsley's nursemaid, and the boy is Richard Pengelly, – 'Old Dick' in the 1930's.)*
My grandfather painted Will Burman in his tiny kitchen which, as we know, fell over the cliff.

1861 *We find a description of Salvation Yeo in Charles Kingsley's "Westward Ho!":-*
"He is a tall man and black. He sweareth awfully, the Lord forgive him."
His father is said to have been a barber, surgeon and preacher. "Yeo" was a liar, but changed his ways later in life and became a Christian. His bowl and watch are in the keeping of Mrs Joan Searles, who is a descendant through the Pengelly family who lived at Providence House. Tom Pengelly was Coxswain 1902-29.

1863/66 *Restoration of All Saints Church. Much good work but unhappily, some "history" destroyed. £300 borrowed from Exeter. £300 raised on rates and much money came in from local efforts.*

1862 *This year, two little girls disappeared from Clovelly, Ellen and Elizabeth Lee, aged 2 and 11 years. Police and villagers looked in vain. Their bodies were found three weeks later in the West Woods, only ½ a mile from their home. (This is a lonely region, reached through the Home Farm and in the direction of Hartland, now private.) A cross was erected over the spot by Mrs Hamlyn in 1902.*

The following was given to me by a friend:-

"Oh, don't you remember – a long time ago,
Those two little babies – their names I don't know.
They strayed away – one bright summer's day,
Those two little babies – got lost on their way.

Now the day being long – and the night coming on,
Those two little babies – sat under a stone,
They sobbed and they sighed – they sat there and cried,
Those two little babies – they lay down and died.

Now the robins so red – how quickly they spread,
They put out their wide wings – and over them spread
And all the day long – in the branches they throng,
They sweetly did whistle – and this was their song.

Chorus: Pretty babes in the wood, pretty babes in the wood. Oh, don't you remember those babes in the wood?"
(A Song For Every Season by Bob Copper and his family).

The lonely woodland cross marks the spot where Ellen and Elizabeth Lee died.

Joseph and Mary Ann Jewell – Survivors of the wreck of "General Grant".

1866 The Loss of the "General Grant."

Joseph Jewell aged 31, and his wife, Mary-Ann aged 21, were on this ill-fated ship. Jo was uncle to Alice, my grandmother. He was serving as an A.B. His wife was a passenger. The ship was new, 1,103 tons, with a cargo of wool, skins, pelts, 9 tons of pelter (thought to have "gold") and two boxes of gold – 2,576 ozs. The cargo was insured for £165,000. Most of the passengers were returning to England carrying quantities of gold – much more than the amount stated.

"The ship sailed from Melbourne on May 4th, 1866, and made good progress until the night of May 13th. The night was dark. The Auckland Islands lay ahead. At 1 a.m., she crashed into a towering cliff and the jib boom was carried away. No-one knew what to do and complete panic overtook the ship. After crashing once, she slowly drifted astern for half a mile where she again struck, losing the rudder. The man at the wheel could do no more, several of his ribs were broken. It seemed as though some malicious fate had overtaken the vessel. She canted on toward the land and finally drifted into a cave about 250 yards deep."

(Shipwrecks – New Zealand Disasters 1795-1950 by Charles Owen Wheatley).

At dawn, steps were taken to land people. Passengers numbered 61, crew 22, but very few landed safely. A chapter of accidents befell them, and only 15 persons actually survived the wreck and settled down to await rescue. Practically all food had been lost, the only clothing was upon their bodies. Seals were captured and eaten, and the skins "sewn" together to form some kind of clothing. For 18 months the poor creatures waited. Four men left in the surviving boat but were never seen again. One man died and so ten remained. A whaling brig found them in 1867 and never was such a group of civilised people seen as this party. Jo and Mary-Ann Jewell were among the ten survivors, and she was the only female.

Joseph and Mary settled in Australia but had no family. She gave lectures on their shipwreck experiences wearing the sealskins made on the Island. Both died in Australia.

1885 Extract from a local paper.

"Will Vine, the baker, and three youths were taking out loaves of bread to a ship in the bay. Their little boat was caught in a big wave by the quay head and all were tipped into the sea. The four were rescued but lost the bread. (Will Vine was the father of 13 children and they lived at No 55, The Wharf.)

1885

"Wm Prince and Wm Jewell were fined 11/6d each at Bideford Magistrates Court on the 14th of April. "Charged with obstruction at Clovelly." P C Kellaway found a net stretched from hedge to hedge touching the ground, just above the Reading Room (No 4 Mount Pleasant.)

"Two lads of Clovelly a-fishing they went,
To catch a red herring it was their intent,
In spreading their net on the side of The Hobby
Unfortunately caught a red-headed bobby!!"

1889 Rev T L V Simkins Notes.

"A vestry meeting was held in the Parish Church at 6 p.m. on 31st October, to consider what course might be thought admirable or to the liability of the parish to repairs and to keep it in repair, it's several streets or highways in the village of Clovelly. Proposed that a request should be laid before the Highway Board, meeting the Board to under-take the repairs of the street leading from the High Street to Fish Street. Also of the severeal highways leading to the different farms in the parish."

The noble body of people dealt with all parish affairs until the first Parish Councils came into being in 1894.

Extracts from early Parish Council minute books.

1894 Dec 4th. First meeting of Clovelly Parish Council held at 6.30 p.m. in the Board School, F Hamlyn in the chair. 17 names nominated, 8 candidates withdrew leaving 9. Names were:- Thomas Andrew, Burnstone; John Andrew, Kennerland; I Baker, Court Farm; Bechalake, Eastacott; Wm Beer, Thorner; Th Cleave, Dyke Farm; Cruse, West Dyke; Wm Cleverdon, Dyke Green; Wm Elliot, Slade; Rev Harrison, Rectory; F Hamlyn, Clovelly Court; Wm Jeffrey, Village; Wm Jewell, Village; Mills, Village; C Prouse, Stitworthy; J Slee, Downland; Mrs Cory, Village.

Proposed Rev Harrison to be Chairman – he declined.

Mr Cruse appointed Chairman. Mr Slee, Clerk. National Provincial Bank, Treasurer. Clerk's salary £1 10s 0d.

Pay Mrs Downing 3/- for lighting school-room, etc.
(Increased to 8/- at next meeting.)

1895 20th April, Mr Hamlyn appointed Chairman at Annual Meeting.
1895 30th June, Election of a local committee for Technical Education = 8 members.
1897 Plans for proposed railway from Bideford to Clovelly put forward.
1898 Mr Hamlyn stated that he had built a mortuary for the use of the parish, free of cost. Vote of thanks.
1903 School Managers appointed in place of Technical representatives.
1904 Death of Mr F Hamlyn.
1908 "The High Street is slippery owing to grease being used on sledges."
1911 Celebrations for Coronation of King George V. 4-11 year olds to receive Coronation Mug. £2 10s 0d allocated. 18/- for Beer. 18/- for Mineral Waters.

Some items of food.

3 round Beef	*£3 7s 6d*
2 roast	*1 7s 0d*
2 Hams	*1 1s 4d*
Cake	*1 17s 0d*
Cut rounds	*1 4s 0d*
Bread	*12s 5d*
Butter	*9s 9d*

32lbs Cream 1/2d lb.

Distribution of Coronation Mugs	–	*Rectory*	*10 a.m.*
Regatta	–	*Quay*	*10-1 p.m.*
Divine Service	–	*Church*	*2.30 p.m.*
Childrens' Sports	–	*Court*	*3.15 p.m.*
Tea	–	*,,*	*4 p.m.*
Adult Sports	–	*,,*	*6 p.m.*
Bonfire	–	*Gallantry Bower*	*10 p.m.*

Donkey-mail – and Mr. Martin the postman.

1926 Donkeys limited to two per man and pay 10/- each for insurance.
1929 Asked for second delivery of mail and that a mail van could bring to top of cobbles to save a man and donkey walking a mile to fetch.
1930 Mr Martin, postman, retired in 1930 after walking 175,000 miles. (Miss M Stevens began the post round in 1918, and received one of the first uniforms.)
List of boarding houses to be compiled to answer visitors' questions. Touting at top to be stopped.
1932 Desirability of a Post Office at Turnpike Gate. Would serve 60 farms and cottages, approximately 200 people. (Many years later, it was opened at Harry Taylor's. Now it is on the turning towards Hartland.)

Here are more extracts from Cory's "Chronicles."

1910 *July 12th. "Three submarines in Clovelly Bay, Nos 24, 30 and 38, with the destroyer "Pembroke." Many visitors rowed round them at anchor. They left next day."*

1910 *Aug 14th. "A dance held at Clovelly Court in aid of the Reading Room. Profit £3 3s 0d."*

1910 *Aug 16th. "Clovelly school-children and others making 200 in all, entertained by Mr & Mrs Basil Heywood of No 104, Clovelly. The full band of the Territorials led the procession to the field. Nuts, fruit, sweets, 3d bits and other presents were given out. All followed the band to the Look-out where selections were played."*

1916 *"Half-year rent audit at Clovelly Estate Office, Oct 21st. Dinner provided by Mrs C Hamlyn. Mr Caird presided. A good time was had by all."*

1918 *"The 'flu epidemic hit Clovelly. 3 deaths. School closed."*

1920 *"War Memorial dedicated to all who fell in the 1914/18 war, was unveiled in Parish Church. Forms brought in as huge congregation. Also blessed a black oak chair given by Mrs Ellis in memory of her husband, John, who had been warden from 1905-1919."*

1920 *June. "North Hill field is beautifully laid out as a memorial to the dead."*

1924 *"New public garages opened." (Now main car park.)*

1925 *"Rose Kingsley died aged 80. Eldest child of Charles Kingsley."*

1925 *"A carved cedar-wood chest, date about 1660, given to Parish Church in memory of Frank Tardivall."*

1927 *"Rechabites and Shipwrecked Mariners processed to New Year's Day Service. Annual meeting after, and dinner at Mary Ann Smale's and Red Lion respectively."*

1929 *"Evelyn Laye visited Clovelly." (The show 'New Moon' produced in London this year.)*

1929 *"The mess in the street is so bad that a special rate of 1d in the £ to pay boys to remove orange peel, cigarette papers and film cartons."*

1929 *"Hartland telephone exchange opened." (10 numbers listed.)*

1932 *"Telephone exchange of the rural automatic type opened at Slerra on March 22nd. Subscribers can dial each other and can obtain Bideford by dialling 01."*

(End of Cory's Chronicles extracts.)

Evelyn Laye at Clovelly, 1929.

1933 *"Rex Whistler designed crockery and material for Mrs Ruthven and Mrs Asquith (nieces of Mrs Hamlyn) – cream background with views of Clovelly in brown, black, blue, green and pink." (Known as Clovelly "Ware" and "Chintz."*

1934 *"Rev P J Somers Cocks formed the Mothers' Union branch in Clovelly."*

1935 *"Coastguard cottages closed. Let to them since 1859."*

1935 *"Mr E Godwin of Burscott, while digging in his neighbour's garden, found a 4½lb. cannon ball, 3" in diameter, which fits the muzzle of the cannons on Clovelly Quay."*

"Mr Godwin picked up a good specimen of a flint barbed arrow-head. From it's size and shape it seems early Bronze Age. During this year, he has collected a number of worked flint flakes, including some borers and scrapers, from the farm, possibly a flint factory."

1936 January. "The Elinor Rogets" final practice after serving Clovelly faithfully for 29 years.
1936 April. 50 local ladies attended a meeting to form a ladies lifeboat guild. It would cost £300 every year to support the new boat.

1936 June 10th. The "City of Nottingham" arrived, – Clovelly's first motor powered lifeboat.
1936 August. "The Elinor Roget" left Clovelly.
1936 November. "Death of Mrs C Hamlyn, aged 80."

1936 "Electricity cables laid under the cobbles in the High Street. 20 local men were employed. Not every cottage took advantage then – those who did paid their own expenses."
1953 "Cobbles removed again for mains water-pipes." (All "mod-cons." but no eye-sores!)
1945-52 Rev A S Chandler, Rector.

He achieved much by forming a branch of the Women's Institute. The Hon Mrs Asquith became first President. From membership numbering 80+ he formed a choir and a drama group. Certificates were gained at several competitions but I am not sure where they rest now. "The Cries of London" in authentic costumes was a great success, too.

A few years before this, a concert party had been active in raising money in and out of the parish. Many years back, Mrs Bushell of the New Inn presented some colourful performances. Mrs Abbott sewed hundreds of costumes for children who took part. All much more fun than pressing a knob on television or radio!

We are almost at the end of our "Interesting Dates." Two are left, and both mean a lot to me. 1974 and 1975. Clovelly became Great Britain's top Floral Village! My proudest moment came when this trophy was presented in London at the "Cafe Royal" – well worth the hours of work and worry we had spent.

We can proudly boast that we won this coveted silver cup for two years running. The South-West Tourist Board Salver bears our name, and we won the "Keep Britain Tidy" Cup. Then in 1975, we received the "Abyss Trophy" for the village, town or city most active in the Britain-in-Bloom effort. All trophies had to be returned, but we have the certificates. In the French competition with 5,000 entries, two-thirds of which were villages, we came in 2nd place and hold a Bronze Medallion, which, with the certificates, is displayed in my "Clovelly Room."

One of Mrs. Buslell's productions.

Clovelly WI Choir 1945-52.

The first Clovelly room had to be dismantled when I discovered what turned out to be "dry-rot" in October of 1981. One day I found a rust coloured dust on each and every surface in the cottage. Slowly but surely this evil fungus had spread under floorboards and through cupboards until the entire rear portion was in a state of collapse, the smell was appalling.

I stuck it out as long as I could but eventually had to move out and down to No 86 – a cottage with doorways of 5½ feet only so that I knocked my head every day. The drains blocked once a week, the lavatory didn't flush and the rayburn chimney had a fault making it unsafe to use!

With my beloved cat "Spock" for company, I spent 20 months there – mainly waiting for the White Cottage to be restored. It was a traumatic experience and something I should not like to repeat. In May of 1984 I returned to live in the cottage once more, beautifully restored by my cousin Alan Johns and his workmen – courtesy of Clovelly Estate Co and T D C. Friends and more cousins helped to redecorate and it soon felt like home again. I duly arranged our family photograhic efforts and grandfathers' water colours in the old shop and now friends and interested people come and browse through my memory collection – some seeking information on old Clovelly residents.

I never thought that I should have to take over where the older folk had left off – they certainly left a large gap when they either moved away to live near their family or sadly died here. It hurts a lot to walk around the village, knowing that all but a few of the people I grew up with are no longer here, I miss their faces and the sound of the soft Clovelly accent. I suppose change comes to every small village, we have been lucky and able to continue in a particular pattern for many decades now. We are in danger of losing two special amenities – the school and the lifeboat – both dear to us. Let's hope that common sense will prevail in both instances.

I must end my story now, I hope dear reader that you have followed through the pages with me. Thankyou.

Sheila A M Ellis.

Clovelly Dance Orchestra about 1929.

"Lenny" Finch, Bunty Caird, Gladys Ellis, Mr Pinnock (Court Butler).